THE Art OF EDITING THE NEWS

THE Art OF

CHILTON BOOK COMPANY
PHILADELPHIA
NEW YORK
LONDON

EDITING THE NEWS

Robert C. McGiffert

Published in Philadelphia by Chilton Book Company
and simultaneously in Ontario, Canada,
by Thomas Nelson & Sons, Ltd.
Manufactured in the United States of America

LIBRARY OF CONGRESS CATALOGING IN
PUBLICATION DATA

McGiffert, Robert C 1922-
The art of editing the news.

1. Journalism—Handbooks, manuals, etc. I. Title.
PN4778.M25 070.4'1 72-5537
ISBN 0-8019-5734-6

To Jackie, Brian, *and* Sarah

Preface

ALTHOUGH I hope this book may be useful to professional newspapermen and women, I have written it primarily for students. I have tried to show, by example, what to do and how to do it. Many of the examples are taken from student newspapers and stories students have written for reporting and editing courses. I have also drawn upon commercial newspapers and have used a few fictitious examples.

I do not intend to promote, attack, or defend single solutions to specific problems of writing and editing. No editor or teacher will agree with everything he reads here, and some, I fear, will disagree often. In newspaper work there is rarely just one "right" way to do something, and I hope that those who disagree on detail will find some merit in the overall philosophy and approach.

Many editors will find the chapter on headlines too rigid, particularly in its opposition to splits of grammatical units and violation of other traditional and (let's face it) arbitrary rules. Actually, I think those who argue that the "split" rules are illogical have a good point. The rules are still observed on most desks, however, so I favor teaching them to students.

The reader may challenge certain points of emphasis—for example, the attention paid to the mechanics of handling quotations, in contrast to the rather brief treatment of libel. I can only reply that this is a text on copy editing, not law, and I must leave the complexities of libel to other writers. The emphasis, by the way, is not what it would have been had I written the manuscript ten years ago, when I left newspaper work to become a teacher. The principles that students find hardest to master are not always the ones I would have expected, and I have tried to be most detailed on the points that have been most troublesome to my students. The book is, in essence, a recapitulation of my courses in copy editing.

I owe particular thanks to my wife, Jackie, who has spent nearly as much time with the manuscript as I have, and who has listened graciously for twenty-five years to nightly harangues about the newsroom and the classroom.

I am also indebted to Warren Brier of the University of Montana and Bill Watt of Lafayette College for their suggestions and comments; to Frank Doyle of the Easton (Pa.) *Express* for the materials he supplied; to the late Hal Kneeland of the *Washington Post* for the things he taught me and the encouragement he gave me; to Paul Barton of Indiana University for helping me become a teacher; and to Ira Harkey, a brave newsman whose example has helped me explain to students what newspaper work is all about.

Missoula, Montana

Contents

Preface xi
The Editor's Job 1
Marking the Copy 3
Identification and Assembly 17
Printing Instructions 33
Leads 38
Story Organization 60
Content 72
Backgrounding 87
Quotations 91
Attribution 103
Grammar 116
The Use and Abuse of Language 129
Wordiness 160
Style, Conventions, and Spelling 174
Cutting for Space 180
Editorializing and Editorials 205
Libel and Fairness 208
Pitfalls 215
Cutlines 225
Headlines 232
A Look at the Future 263

THE Art OF EDITING THE NEWS

The Editor's Job

THE newspaper copy editor, known by newsmen as the copyreader, has three jobs: to improve copy, to tell the printer how to assemble stories and what type to use, and to write headlines.

He works with a soft pencil, eraser, scissors (or ruler), and paste.

Ideally, he has an ear for language, alertness, an inquiring mind, news judgment, broad general knowledge, and a desire for perfection.

His ear for language detects awkward, unclear, dull, trite, and ungrammatical writing.

His alertness protects his newspaper from inaccuracy, partiality, ridicule, and libel suits.

His inquiring mind seeks answers to questions the reporter has overlooked.

His news judgment helps him bring out the best in a story.

His general knowledge helps him spot the false, the incomplete, and the misleading.

His desire for perfection gives him the will to improve the inadequate story even when he is tired and time is short and a voice is whispering that the reader won't care.

The beginner must understand that even a skilled reporter usually needs editing.

"He that pleads his own cause has a fool for a client" goes an English proverb. A like principle applies to writing. The reporter who has no editor is heading for trouble.

The writer is too close to his work to judge it. He has a psychological blind spot for his own error, omission, and discordant phrase.

The newspaper reporter is particularly myopic. Because of deadline pressure, he can seldom put a story aside and come back to it later, refreshed. His first draft is his last. He makes corrections and improvements as soon as he has finished writing, while his mind is still fixed in its writing pattern.

The copyreader has not had the problem of creation. He brings a fresh viewpoint to the story. He is in a better position than the writer to spot the cliché, the inconsistency, the muddy phrase, the omission, the redundancy.

The copyreader suspects every story of being badly organized, inaccurate, incomplete, biased, misleading, uninteresting, unfair, and full of errors in grammar, usage, and spelling. Yet he recognizes the story that is none of these things, and has the good sense to leave it alone.

On a weekly newspaper, the copyreader may be the editor and publisher and even reporter, all rolled into one. On a small-city daily, he may be the city editor or the telegraph editor or the state editor. On a metropolitan newspaper, he may have no responsibility other than reading copy and writing heads. Regardless of his title and assignments, his function as copyreader does not change. He is generally the last editorial department employee to see a story. He stands between the reporter and the reader. Whatever flaws he doesn't see, the subscriber does.

The copyreader judges his own work as harshly as he judges each reporter's. He checks his editing before he passes a story on. If error or bad writing appears in the paper, he holds himself responsible.

Experienced golfers don't have to remind themselves to look at the ball and keep the left arm straight, and experienced copyreaders don't keep a list of dos and don'ts in front of them for reference. But just as Nicklaus and Palmer and Trevino once had to think consciously about techniques, so does the beginning copyreader have to check each story point by specific point. He must ask himself these questions:

(1) Is the story grammatical?
(2) Does it conform to style?
(3) Is it consistent?
(4) Is it accurate?
(5) Is it complete?
(6) Does it have the right lead?
(7) Is it well organized?
(8) Is it fair?
(9) Is it objective?
(10) Is it in good taste?
(11) Is it clear?
(12) Is it concise?
(13) Is everything spelled right?
(14) Am I sure about all the names?
(15) Have I checked all dates and numbers?
(16) Have I deleted anything that I should restore?

If he is satisfied on these points, the editor is ready to move on to the next story.

Marking The Copy

IN PREPARING copy, the editor uses symbols known as copyreading marks. These show the compositor where paragraphs begin and where changes must be made. Here are the basic marks, with illustrations of how they are used:

start a paragraph	The next step
capitalize (put in upper case)	phoenix, ariz.
change to small letter (lower case)	a Bear bit him
insert letter	rocket lunching (a)
insert word	his boots saddle (and)
change letter	stationary store (e)
change word	large but nasty (and)
delete letter	a books of matches
delete letter and close up	lunnatic fringe
delete word or words	too very bad
delete punctuation	Munson, of Detroit
transpose letters	he flet homesick

	transpose words	a foreign black car
#	separate	stormyweather
	close up	false pre mise
	insert period	It was the end
	insert comma	It was he said the end.
	insert apostrophe	took Smiths place
	begin quotation	She said, Look here, I
	end quotation	think you're mean.
	delete, run lines together (run in)	snow fell from up there out of sight in the somber sky
	delete paragraph	The patrolman said that if the crash had actually occurred, someone might have been hurt.
	change style to:	
	spelling	Main St.
	abbreviation	Lansing, Michigan
	spelling	3 days ago
	numeral	fourteen acres
# -30- ///	end mark	#

There are minor variations in the use of marks. Some newspapers designate paragraphs this way: ¶ . Some indicate capitals with one underline instead of three. Some use a wavy underline to order italics or boldface type. Other symbols have been devised to take care of particular local needs. The marks reproduced here meet most of the requirements of most newspapers, however. To see how they do their job, let's look at a story before and after it has been edited.

smith

robbery

Two young women used a knife to hold up a small market tuesday night several hours after four men wearing stokcing caps rob bed another store at gunpoint.

The 2 women took $102 from tge Front Street Market 498 Front Street, and the three men took approximately $250 from the Zieglerand Kline Market, Pomfret Ave. and Belleeview Blvd.

The two unscrupulous women who rabbed thw Front street store were described as Caucasians between eighteen and 22 years old. They wearing short green coats. The cleerk at the store, Harriet Milton, said: They looked enough alike, to be sis-ters"

The three chaps who robbed the Pomfret Ave. store so brazenly were descibred as negroes

17 in their late 20's, two of them tall and slender,
18 the Other short and fat.
19 One customer described the short, fat man
20 as "incredibly handsome," but another said all three
21 men were "incredibly ugly."
22 The owner of the store Imogene Markup, said
23 she and her 17 year old daughter, Priscilla, were
24 alone in the store before the men entered at six
25 p.m. One drew a pistol, she said, and only spoke
26 one word: "Stickup.
27 "They didnt tell me to lie on the floor or
28 anything", said she with a chuckle.
29 One of the other men, a very mean fellow
30 indeed, to judge from the conduct and attitude
31 reported by Mrs. Markup, then made an unsuccessful
32 attempt to open the cash register.
33

Now let's go back over the story, line by line, and note what the copyreader must do with it.

First he'll line out the reporter's name (Smith) and underline the identifying word, or "slug" (robbery). Now to the story itself:

Line 1: Mark the paragraph
Line 2: Capitalize t in "tuesday"
Line 3: Transpose letters in "stokcing," close up "rob bed"
Line 4: Mark the paragraph, spell 2, fix "tge"
Line 5: Insert comma after "Market," abbreviate "Street"

Line 6:	Change "approximately" to "about," separate "Zieglerand"
Line 7:	Spell out "Ave." and "Blvd.," delete extra e in "Belleeview"
Line 8:	Indicate more to come
Line 9:	Mark paragraph, delete "unscrupulous," fix "rabbed" and "thw"
Line 10:	Capitalize s in "street"
Line 11:	Change "eighteen" to 18, insert "were"
Line 12:	Fix "cleerk"
Line 13:	Insert quotation mark, delete comma
Line 14:	Insert period
Line 15:	Mark paragraph, change "chaps" to "men"
Line 16:	Spell out "Ave.," delete "so brazenly," fix "descibred," capitalize n in "negroes"
Line 17:	Delete apostrophe
Line 18:	Put O in lower case
Lines 19–21:	Delete paragraph
Line 22:	Mark paragraph, insert comma
Line 23:	Insert hyphens
Line 24:	Change "before" to "when," change "six" to 6
Line 25:	Transpose "only spoke"
Line 26:	Insert quotation mark
Line 27:	Mark paragraph, insert apostrophe
Line 28:	Transpose punctuation, transpose "said she," delete "with a chuckle"
Line 29:	Mark paragraph, begin deletion
Line 30:	Continue deletion
Line 31:	Complete deletion
Line 32:	Insert attribution
Line 33:	Insert end mark

Here's how the story looks now:

~~smith~~

robbery

Two young women used a knife to hold up a small market tuesday night several hours after four men wearing stokcing caps rob bed another store at gunpoint.

The 2 women took $102 from tae Front Street Market 498 Front Street, and the three men took approximately $250 from the Zieglerand Kline Market, Pomfret Ave. and Belleview Blvd.

The two unscrupulous women who rabbed tha Front street store were described as Caucasians between eighteen and 22 years old. They wearing short green coats. The cleerk at the store, Harriet Milton, said: They looked enough alike to be sis-ters

The three chaps who robbed the Pomfret Ave. store so brazenly were descibred as negroes in their late 20's, two of them tall and slender, the other short and fat.

One customer described the short, fat man as "incredibly handsome," but another said all three men were "incredibly ugly."

The owner of the store Imogene Markup, said she and her 17 year old daughter, Priscilla, were alone in the store before the men entered at six p.m. One drew a pistol, she said, and only spoke one word: "Stickup."

"They didn't tell me to lie on the floor or anything", ~~said she with a chuckle.~~ she said.

One of the other men, ~~a very mean fellow indeed, to judge from the conduct and attitude reported by Mrs. Markup,~~ then made an unsuccessful attempt to open the cash register, according to Mrs. Markup.

\#

Copyreading marks should speed production, not delay it, so if there is any danger of confusion the copyreader should ignore the symbol and make the change by lining out the bad material and writing in the good. In line 16, for example, "descibred" would look like this if it were repaired with symbols:

descibred

That's pretty messy, so it is better to make the correction this way:

described ~~descibred~~

Similarly, line 28 could be made to look like this:

anything", said she, ~~with a chuckle.~~

This is better:

anything", she said. ~~said she with a chuckle.~~

The beginner is sure to do things that will puzzle the compositor. Here are some of them, with suggestions for clear marking:

(1) In transposing letters, use the symbol only for a simple switch of two adjacent letters. Otherwise, line out and write in.

Do not do this:

Connectutic   adnimistration

Instead, do this:

Connectutic (icut)   adnimistration (m, n)

Or this:

(connecticut) ~~Connectutic~~   (administration) ~~adnimistration~~

(2) In transposing groups of words, do not use the symbol when the change involves interior correction of punctuation and capitalization.

Do not do this:

Tired, sick and hungry was the dog.

Instead, do this:

(The dog was)
Tired, sick and hungry ~~was the dog.~~

(3) Do not use the transposition symbol when the change involves the first word of a sentence.

Do not do this:

For the good of the team he quit.

Instead, do this:

(He quit)
For the good of the team ~~he quit.~~

(4) In deleting or inserting a word that is preceded or followed by punctuation, move the punctuation to its logical position. If you don't, the compositor may insert a space before he sees the punctuation.

Do not do this:

She stumbled twice ~~but did not fall~~.

Instead, do this:

She stumbled twice ~~but did not fall~~.

Do not do this:

> First
> ~~Initially~~, last and always.

Instead, do this:

> First,
> ~~Initially,~~ last and always.

Do not do this:

> broke the
> Harry Harpoon, abalone hunter~~, set a~~ record.

Instead, do this:

> broke the
> Harry Harpoon, abalone hunter, ~~set a~~ record.

Do not do this:

> Copperstone said: "~~Ladies and gentlemen,~~ I
>
> am extremely proud to be a moderate."

Instead, do this:

> "
> Copperstone said: ~~"Ladies and gentlemen,~~ I
>
> am extremely proud to be a moderate."

(5) Guard against destroying punctuation with editing marks.

Do not do this:

> He returned to Pascagoula, Mississippi his
>
> home town.

Instead, do this:

> He returned to Pascagoula, Mississippi, his
>
> home town.

(6) Do not use a symbol when the change involves more than one line.

Do not do this:

He was an employee of the National

Aeronautics and Space Administration.

Instead, do this:

He was an employee of ~~the National~~

~~Aeronautics and Space Administration.~~

Do not do this:

He worked for the Department of Education,

Health and Welfare.

Instead, do this:

He worked for the Department of ~~Education,~~

~~Health~~ and Welfare.

(7) Do not use circles and arrows to indicate a change in position of a word, phrase, or paragraph.

Do not do this:

As night fell, ~~he~~ realized that he was lost

in the woods, and Harkey decided to make camp.

Instead, do this:

As night fell, ~~he~~ realized that he was lost

in the woods, and ~~Harkey~~ decided to make camp.

(8) To change the position of an entire paragraph or more, cut the copy apart, then paste the paragraphs together in proper order.

Do not do this:

Barney Laeufer won first place in the fat
lamb competition.

Campbell Titchener was named grand champion
showman.

Instead, do this:

Campbell Titchener was named grand champion
showman.

Barney Laeufer won first place in the fat
lamb competition.

(9) Do not "stack" lines of handwritten changes on top of each other. Keep the inserted material on a single plane, letting the corrections run to the next line of copy if necessary.

Do not do this:

was serving a prison term and therefore

Norton pointed out that he couldn't have been
in the store at the time of the shooting.

Instead, do this:

was serving a prison term

Norton pointed out that he ~~couldn't have been~~

and therefore couldn't have been

in the store at the time of the shooting.

(10) Since the purpose of a close-up symbol over a deletion is to carry the typesetter's eye from one word to the next, do not use the mark when

the deletion comes at the end or beginning of a line. Use the run-in symbol instead.

Do not do this:

```
        Pronounced unfit by Dr. Herman Catapult, ~~a~~
    ~~specialist in dog diseases with offices on Russell~~,
    were three horses entered by Mrs. Harold L. Perverse.
```

Instead, do this:

```
        Pronounced unfit by Dr. Herman Catapult, ~~a~~
    ~~specialist in dog diseases with offices on Russell,~~
    were three horses entered by Mrs. Harold L. Perverse.
```

And there's no point in getting fancy, like this:

```
        Pronounced unfit by Dr. Herman Catapult, ~~a~~
    ~~specialist in dog diseases with offices on Russell,~~
    were three horses entered by Mrs. Harold L. Perverse.
```

(11) Do not use the run-in mark when a new paragraph follows a deletion. (Run-in means "don't indent," and the two marks would therefore conflict with each other.)

Do not do this:

```
    . . . went to the house to check, but found no
    one there.
        ~~Neighbors confirmed the fact that Mr. and~~
    ~~Mrs. Hunter had been vacationing for several weeks~~.
        When he returned to the store, he said,
    he telephoned police.
```

Instead, do this:

. . . went to the house to check, but found no one there.

~~Neighbors confirmed the fact that Mr. and Mrs. Hunter had been vacationing for several weeks.~~

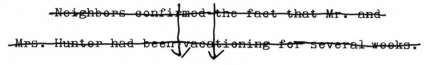

When he returned to the store, he said, he telephoned police.

(12) When deleting at the start of the paragraph, move the paragraph mark to the right.

Do not do this:

~~The victims, Sigmund~~ O'Toole and ~~Sean~~ Schultz, were taken . . .

Instead, do this:

~~The victims, Sigmund~~ O'Toole and ~~Sean~~ Schultz, were taken . . .

(13) Write in punctuation at the proper level.

Do not do this:

The medical examiner, Dr. Harry Turner, said . . .

Instead, do this:

The medical examiner, Dr. Harry Turner, said . . .

(14) Be neat. Put marks in the right place.

Do not do this:

[the nomination]
He won on ~~the third~~ ballot, after gaining

strength on the second.

Instead, do this:

[the nomination]
He won on the third ballot, after gaining

strength on the second.

(15) Line out and write in neatly.

Do not do this.

[scored on the next play.]
Hummingbird ~~lugged the spheroid into TD land~~

~~on the next slant.~~

Instead, do this:

[scored on the next play.]
Hummingbird ~~lugged the spheroid into TD land~~

~~on the next slant.~~

On most newspapers, reporters are told not to break words at the end of a line and not to end a page in the middle of a paragraph. They still do it, though. The copyreader should fix the broken word by writing it all on one line or the other, and should use the most convenient method—paste pot and shears, typewriter, or longhand—to fix paragraphs that break from one page to the next.

Some newsrooms avoid the paragraph break by pasting the multipage story together into one long strip of copy. It is then up to the copycutter, a composing room employee, to cut it into lengths that are convenient for typesetting.

Identification And Assembly

LIKE physical evidence at a trial, newspaper copy must be "marked for identification" so that the news and composing rooms can keep track of it. The label on the copy is a descriptive word or two placed in the upper left corner of the page. It is called a "slug."

On a football practice story, the slug might be "gridders"; on a story about parietal rules, it might be "dorm hours." The slug may be one word or several, according to the practice of the newspaper, but regardless of the style it must be distinctive enough to apply to only one story in a given issue.

The bigger the paper, the more care must be taken to avoid the duplication of slugs. The word "accident" might be a safe slug for a six-page campus newspaper that rarely carries an accident story, but it would be too commonplace for a metropolitan daily.

The slug serves several purposes:

It saves time. The deskman who calls the composing room about a missing proof need not say, "Al, I need a proof of the story about the woman who spent two thousand bucks to find her lost cat." All he need say is, "Al, I need a proof of 'catlover.' "

It guides the printer who assembles the type. (For this reason the slug is sometimes called a "guideline.") The story and its headline are usually set in type at different times on different machines, and must be matched later. A story may go to the composing room in sections, called "takes," and the takes must be arranged in sequence. Events may affect a story after it has gone to the compositor, and the additions, deletions, insertions, revisions, and corrections must be made at the right places in the type. It is the slug that tells the printer what headline goes with what story, and where to put the various pieces of the story.

It is essential in makeup. Whether he creates a page by putting type into a page form, as in letterpress printing, or by making a pasteup of the page, as in offset lithography, the printer follows a layout sheet that shows him where stories, headlines, and pictures are to go. These components are identified by their slugs.

Normally, it is not up to the copyreader to decide what slug to put on a story. That is the job of the news editor or another editor with makeup responsibilities. The copyreader must check to see that the story has been slugged, however, and if it hasn't been he must find out what the slug should be and write it in.

Some copy desks use the first word or two of the headline as the slug. This works as long as the head can be written before the story goes to the composing room. If the story moves first, though, it must be slugged without regard to the language of the headline, and when the head is written the slug must be changed to conform to it. That means extra steps. The system also increases the danger of duplicating a slug. Stories headed "Two Men Pass State Bar Exams" and "Two Men Arrested for Drunken Driving" might both be slugged "Two Men,"and if the stories are carried in the same section or department it is an even-money bet that the heads will be reversed.

The copy usually includes the page number or department where the story is to be carried, however, which lessens the danger of such a mix-up. Even though they have the same slug, the stories and their heads can be told apart by the additional information.

When an issue carries several related stories, grouped on one page or in one section, the copy may bear a general "key" in addition to the slug. A story for a special section on college commencement activities, for example, might look like this in the upper left corner:

```
jones
key graduation
slug senior prom
page 22
```

The key is generally used only on feature material prepared well in advance of publication. Its main purpose is to help the composing room to keep track of type stored on galleys for future use.

The slug is to a story what the surname is to a family. It is basic identification of a whole, and applies to all the parts. If the first take of a story is slugged "Senior Prom," subsequent takes will be Senior Prom "adds." Some offices mark these "add 1 Senior Prom" and "add 2 Senior Prom," or "1st add Senior Prom" and "2nd add Senior Prom." Others simply number the takes consecutively, such as "Senior Prom 1;" "Senior Prom 2," and "Senior Prom 3."

A paragraph inserted in the body of a story is called an insert. If there is only one, it can be slugged "Insert Senior Prom." If there are two or more, each must have a letter or a number: "A insert Senior Prom," "B insert Senior Prom," "1st insert Senior Prom," "Senior Prom 1st insert," and the like.

The copyreader must tell the printer where to insert the new material. Sometimes he knows in advance that an insert will be needed, and can indicate it on the copy by writing "insert coming" or "TR for insert." More often, though, he can't foresee the insert and must show on a galley proof where it goes, or point the spot out, in person, to the printer.

The letters "TR "means "turn rule." A rule is a piece of type metal that makes a solid line to separate columns and stories or to set off pictures. Like the type face, it stands in relief on a metal base or slug. The base is wider than the printing surface. When the rule is turned upside down, it prints as a heavy black band. (A paper that frames a page with a mourning band is said to have "turned its rules.") A turned rule is easy to spot in a galley or a page of type and is a convenient device for attracting the printer's attention.

When the copyreader handles an insert that has not been indicated on the original copy, he takes a galley proof of the story, writes "insert" or "TR for insert" in the margin, and uses an arrow or wedge to show where the new material is to go.

Deletions, called "kills," may be required after the copy has gone to the composing room. Unless he can call the story back before it is set in type, the copyreader must mark kills on the proof. If less than a paragraph is to be killed, he lines out the material and uses the proofreader's delete symbol (₰) in the margin. If he is killing a whole paragraph or a group of paragraphs, he pencils a box around the material, puts an "X" through it, and writes "kill" in the margin, encircling the word and running an arrow or wedge from it to the deletion.

Once the type has been set, the copyreader can make minor changes by marking the proof. If he is revising a substantial part of a paragraph, however, he kills the entire original paragraph on the proof, types the revised paragraph as a separate take, slugs it as an insert, and indicates on the proof that an insert is coming. On some papers a replacement paragraph of this sort is marked "sub for kill" rather than "insert."

A new lead is handled the same way. The copyreader puts an "X" through the original lead on the proof and writes "kill—new lead coming." On the fresh copy, he writes "new lead" next to the slug or under it.

When a story goes to the composing room without a lead, the copyreader writes "lead to kum" or "LTK" next to the slug. The letters "HTK" mean "head to kum" and are used to advise the composing room of a delay in a headline.

The copyreader must mark the end as well as the beginning of the story and each of its parts.

At the bottom of the last take, he uses the end mark: # or 30.

When a page ends and there is more to come, he writes "more."

At the end of an insert, he writes either "end insert" or "TR for pick." (Here "pick" means "pickup" and tells the printer he must "pick up" more type.)

If the insert has two or more takes, he can write "more" on the first take and slug the additional takes "add insert." However, it is safer if he treats the takes as separate inserts and letters or numbers them consecutively.

At the end of a new lead, he writes "end new lead" or "TR for pick."

If the new lead has two or more takes, he writes "more" on the first take and slugs the others as adds. On the last take of the new lead, he writes "TR for pick" and then marks the proof of the original type as an add, in its sequence.

It is assumed that copy is for the current issue unless otherwise specified. The copyreader who handles advances must make sure the day of publication is written on the copy, or that it is marked "hold for release."

Copy written in advance as "add matter" pending development of a basic story is known variously as "B copy," "X copy," "A copy," or just "add copy." It might be biographical material for use in an obituary, or background information on a bill coming up for debate, or the history of a building that is scheduled for demolition. If the material is to be used in the current issue, the copyreader writes "lead to kum" under the slug. If the date of use is uncertain, he writes "hold for release."

While all this may seem complex, the system is essentially simple, and the copyreader who understands the logic of it can make himself understood in any composing room, regardless of local variations in vocabulary and mechanics. All he is doing, really, is getting the segments of type lined up in proper order, and if he gives instructions clearly, on the copy and on the proof, he should have no trouble.

Few stories involve all the procedures just outlined, so let's look at a hypothetical one that does, and see how the copyreader might handle it.

Let's assume that you are a copyreader on the *Gazette*, an afternoon daily in the city of Eastport. The Eastport City Council is scheduled to meet at 11 a.m. today.

The City Hall reporter has until 2:30 p.m. to complete his story for the final city edition, but there are two earlier editions, delivered in rural communities and the suburbs, and the deadline for the first of these is 11:30.

Before he leaves the office, the City Hall man, Ed Smith, writes this tentative story for the first edition:

smith
zoning

An ordinance that would make 27 changes in the Eastport zoning code was scheduled for introduction at a meeting of the City Council today.

The changes are supported by the Eastport Taxpayers League but are opposed by the Civic Betterment Association and several service clubs.

The legislation was expected to produce a sharp debate between Councilmen Ladislav McGurk and Hans Botticelli.

McGurk is the sponsor of the ordinance. Botticelli, who has consistently opposed changes in zoning, charged last week that the measure would turn the North Side into "a vast wasteland of saloons, rendering plants and abattoirs."

Smith says he will call before deadline if there is any change; since the story is short and will not tax the typesetting facilities, the copy is held at the city desk pending his call.

Shortly after eleven, Smith reports that the ordinance has been introduced. You change "was scheduled for introduction" to "was introduced," and send the story to the composing room after slugging it this way:

smith
zoning
HTK
PTD

"PTD" means "proof to desk." Although it is standard procedure to send proofs to the newsroom, the "PTD" adds a little insurance. It means that an extra proof will be pulled, and it warns the composing room that "slug zoning" will probably be changed before makeup time.

When the type has been set, the proof looks like this:

ZONING - HTK - PTD

An ordinance that would make 27 changes in the Eastport zoning code was introduced at a meeting of the City Council today.

The changes are supported by the Eastport Taxpayers

League but are opposed by the Civic Betterment Association and several service clubs.

The legislation was expected to produce a sharp debate between Councilmen Ladislav McGurk and Hans Botticelli.

McGurk is the sponsor of the ordinance. Botticelli, who has consistently opposed changes in zoning, charged last week that the measure would turn the North Side into "a vast wasteland of saloons, rendering plants and abattoirs."

While the compositor has been setting this material in type, there have been developments at City Hall. Smith has called a rewrite man and told him that McGurk and Botticelli have been snapping at each other, as predicted. The rewrite man writes this:

Councilmen Ladislav McGurk and Hans Botticelli argued bitterly, as expected, as soon as the measure reached the floor. Because both shouted at once, spectators were unable to distinguish their words.

You mark the new copy this way:

Insert zoning

Councilmen Ladislav McGurk and Hans Botticelli argued bitterly, as expected, as soon as the measure reached the floor. Because both shouted at once, spectators were unable to distinguish their words.

TR for pick

Then you take the proof, write "CX" (for "corrections") to show that it must be corrected, and substitute the new paragraph for the one that has been superseded, like this:

ZONING - HTK - PTD (Cx)

An ordinance that would make 27 changes in the Eastport zoning code was introduced at a meeting of the City Council today.

The changes are supported by the Eastport Taxpayers League but are opposed by the Civic Betterment Association and several service clubs.

The legislation was expected to produce a sharp debate between Councilmen Ladislav McGurk and Hans Botticelli. (Kill) Insert

McGurk is the sponsor of the ordinance. Botticelli, who has consistently opposed changes in zoning, charged last week that the measure would turn the North Side into "a vast wasteland of saloons, rendering plants and abattoirs."

While you have been marking the proof, Smith has called again, and the rewrite man has typed this new lead:

An ordinance that amends the Eastport zoning code in 27 places was passed by a 5-2 vote of the City Council today.

You take the copy and mark it this way:

new lead zoning

An ordinance that amends the Eastport zoning code in 27 places was passed by a 5-2 vote of the City Council today.

(TR for pick)

Then you take the proof, mark in the new lead, and change the tense in the second and fourth paragraphs to conform with the new development:

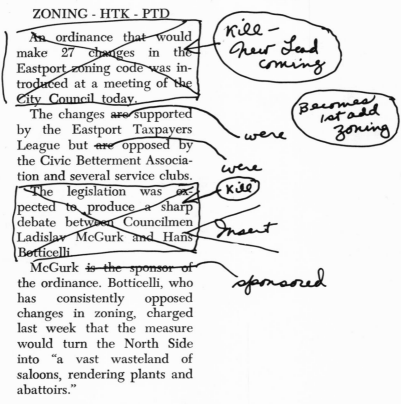

ZONING - HTK - PTD

An ordinance that would make 27 changes in the Eastport zoning code was introduced at a meeting of the City Council today.

Kill — new lead coming

The changes are supported by the Eastport Taxpayers League but are opposed by the Civic Betterment Association and several service clubs.

were were

Becomes 1st add zoning

The legislation was expected to produce a sharp debate between Councilmen Ladislav McGurk and Hans Botticelli.

Kill Insert

McGurk is the sponsor of the ordinance. Botticelli, who has consistently opposed changes in zoning, charged last week that the measure would turn the North Side into "a vast wasteland of saloons, rendering plants and abattoirs."

sponsored

Now it's only a couple of minutes before deadline, and the rewrite man has handled the last call that Smith can make for the first edition. He has written the following, as an add:

```
     The Council adjourned immediately after the
vote.  Members were scheduled to attend a party
at the new OK Lounge on the North Side prior to
groundbreaking ceremonies on the site of a new
slaughterhouse next door.
```

You take the copy and mark it this way:

2nd add zoning

```
     The Council adjourned immediately after the
vote.  Members were scheduled to attend a party
at the new OK Lounge on the North Side prior to
groundbreaking ceremonies on the site of a new
slaughterhouse next door.
```

#

Then you take the proof and show that an add is coming, like this:

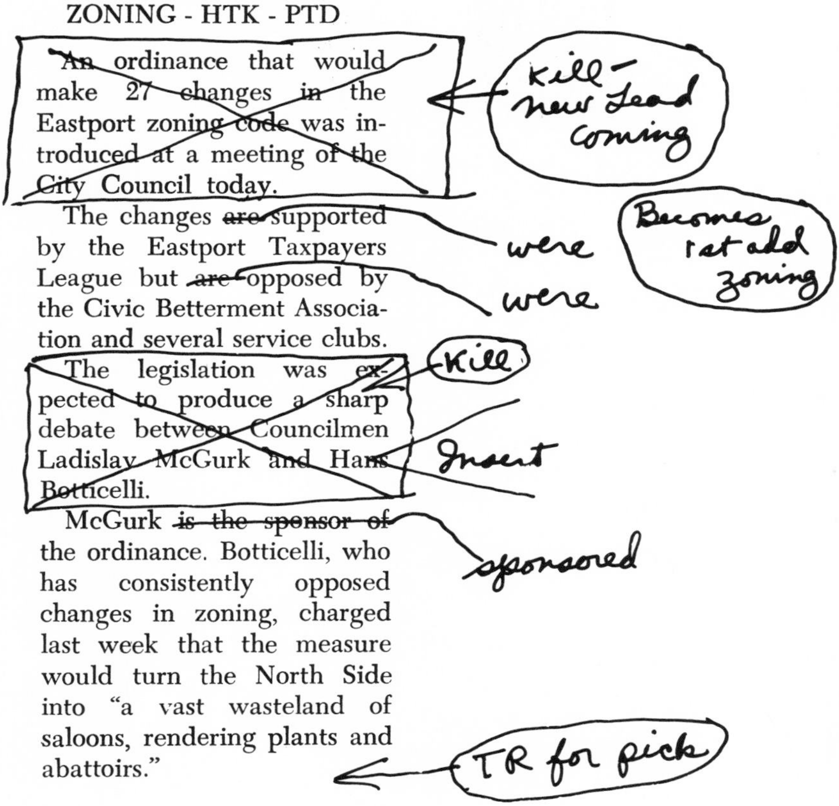
ZONING - HTK - PTD

~~An ordinance that would make 27 changes in the Eastport zoning code was introduced at a meeting of the City Council today.~~

The changes ~~are~~ supported by the Eastport Taxpayers League but ~~are~~ opposed by the Civic Betterment Association and several service clubs.

~~The legislation was expected to produce a sharp debate between Councilmen Ladislav McGurk and Hans Botticelli.~~

McGurk ~~is the sponsor of~~ the ordinance. Botticelli, who has consistently opposed changes in zoning, charged last week that the measure would turn the North Side into "a vast wasteland of saloons, rendering plants and abattoirs."

Now you send the proof back to the composing room, and if all has gone well the story in the first edition will look like this:

An ordinance that amends the Eastport zoning code in 27 places was passed by a 5-2 vote of the City Council today.

The changes were supported by the Eastport Taxpayers League but were opposed by the Civic Betterment Association and several service clubs.

Councilmen Ladislav McGurk and Hans Botticelli argued bitterly, as expected, as soon as the measure reached the floor. Because both shouted at once, spectators were unable to distinguish their words.

McGurk sponsored the ordinance. Botticelli, who has consistently opposed changes in zoning, charged last week that the measure would turn the North Side into "a vast wasteland of saloons, rendering plants and abattoirs."

The Council adjourned immediately after the vote. Members were scheduled to attend a party at the new OK Lounge on the North Side prior to ground-breaking ceremonies on the site of a new slaughterhouse next door.

Basically, wire copy is handled the same way as local. There are differences only in detail. Although teletype machines can print in both upper and lower case, some news wires are "all cap," printing only capital letters. The copyreader handling an all-cap wire must underline all letters that he wants capitalized.

He must also make the dateline conform to his paper's style. (The term "dateline" is often a misnomer, since the line may designate only the story's point of origin, and not the date. This is true particularly on afternoon papers.) The style varies widely, but the traditional design remains the most common: the dateline is indented like a paragraph, the name of the city is in upper case, the name of the state or country is in capitals and lower case, the wire service credit is in parentheses.

Except for the U.S.S.R., the country's name is usually spelled out, but the name of the state is abbreviated in accordance with the paper's style book. If the date is used, it follows the name of the point of origin. The wire service designation, in parentheses, comes next, with no intervening punctuation other than the period required by the abbreviation. After that there's a dash, and then the story begins.

Most papers drop the name of the state on "in-state" stories, but make exceptions to avoid confusion. There are "Washingtons," for example, in 25 states and Puerto Rico, in addition to the District of Columbia, so even an Oklahoma newspaper would dateline a story "WASHINGTON, Okla." rather than "WASHINGTON" alone.

The names of well-known capitals and other major cities can also stand alone in datelines. Most newspapers would not add the country or state to such place names as Buenos Aires, Berlin, Hong Kong, Cairo, London, Paris, Calcutta, Los Angeles, Chicago, Philadelphia, San Francisco, Washington (if it's D.C.), New York, and Detroit.

Here are some typical datelines:

```
KINGSPORT, Tenn. (AP)—

SAN FRANCISCO, July 26 (UPI)—

NICE, France, Sept. 6 (UPI)—

SIOUX CITY, Iowa (Special)—

NEW DELHI  (Reuter)—
```

There are exceptions (the *San Francisco Chronicle* carries the dateline above the body type, and on inside pages uses the wire service credit as a kind of signature, at the end of the story), but in most offices the dateline and wire service credit run directly into the text of the story, without paragraphing. The beginning copyreader sometimes makes this error:

```
NEW YORK (AP)—A man who

said he had just arrived from Mars

was taken into custody by police

in Central Park today.
```

The correct marking is this:

```
NEW YORK (AP)—A man who

said he had just arrived from Mars

was taken into custody by police

in Central Park today.
```

The beginner may also be tempted to add unnecessary punctuation, like this:

```
DOVER, N.H. (UPI)—A man
who said his brother was overdue
in Dover on a trip from Mars was
picked up by the police today.
```

The correct marking is this:

```
DOVER, N.H. (UPI)—A man
who said his brother was overdue
in Dover on a trip from Mars was
picked up by the police today.
```

Wire stories filed by AP and UPI are usually slugged for identification, although the slug is sometimes omitted on routine stories carried on regional or state wires.

Teletype copy also carries a number of symbols. These vary with the wire service, the region, the point of origin, and the nature of the material carried on the particular wire, but generally the symbols are used to identify the wire, the point of origin, and the teletype operator, and they give the story's file number (called a "book number"), its length, the number of takes expected, the date, and the time the transmission begins or ends.

The AP national trunk wire, for example, is the "A" wire, while the New Jersey wire is the "C" wire. The 53rd item filed on the A wire during a given 12-hour transmission cycle would be A053 and the sixth item on the New Jersey wire would be C6.

The operator's initials and the date and time are sometimes at the top of the item, like this:

```
jw203aed 8-5
```

Translated, this means that J. W. began sending the story at 2:03 a.m., Eastern Daylight time, on August 5. Or the information can appear at the end of the item, like this:

```
DM805pcs March 3
```

This means that D. M. completed the transmission at 8:05 p.m., Central Standard time, on March 3.

Most of the information conveyed by the symbols on the wire is for record-keeping purposes, and except for the book number is rarely of much concern to the individual newspaper. The book number is useful as a reference point when the paper questions the wire service about a fact, or wants additional information, or needs a repeat of an item that has been garbled or not received. Mostly, though, the symbols simply get lined out at the copy desk.

Teletypesetter circuits (TTS) make it possible for linecasting and photocomposing machines to set type automatically, without manual operation. A keyboard similar to that of the standard teletype sending machine is used to punch a tape, and the tape is then fed into the machine much as a roll is fed into a player piano.

Less skill and training are required to operate a perforating keyboard than a Linotype machine, and many newspapers set type on their own TTS systems. The wire services also supply copy by TTS. On these circuits, "reperforators" in the newspaper's composing room punch tape in response to electrical impulses, while the news department simultaneously receives the printed story on teletype machines known as "monitors." Monitors print in upper and lower case on paper only six inches wide, as opposed to eight on all-cap wires. They print symbols similar to those carried on other wire service teletypes, and in addition have what is called a "junk" line. When it is received electronically by the reperforator, the junk line punches a book number into the tape visually, so that when the telegraph editor tells the composing room he wants "HN94" set in type the printer can spot it by the  at the top of the roll of tape. The junk line appears on the monitor (as yyruivee, or some such) but is of no concern to the copy desk.

A paper that is not equipped for automatic composition may still receive some or all of its wire service copy on TTS monitors rather than "wide copy" machines, and a paper that is fully automated may edit wire copy in the traditional way before putting it on tape. In either case, the copyreaders handle the TTS monitor material the same as any other. (They must, however, mark in all parentheses. The TTS system can instruct the typecasting machine to set parentheses, but it can't make the monitors print them.)

When a newspaper uses wire service tape to set type automatically, any editing it does requires that type be reset, usually by manual operation. This is time-consuming and costly, and many papers therefore limit their editing of TTS to kills of whole paragraphs. Since wire services can be as guilty of poor editing as anyone else, a lot of bad copy that might have been fixed in the old days is getting into print these days.

Because they serve many newspapers, meeting an almost infinite number of deadlines, the major wire services file lots of adds, inserts, new leads, and revisions. They identify these story fragments precisely, noting how they fit together. The language used is similar to the copy desk vocabulary discussed earlier in this chapter. The instructions are for the use of editors rather than printers, however, and it is up to the copyreader to slug the copy for the composing room.

In filing an add to a story, the wire service normally identifies the basic story by dateline, book number, and slug, and as insurance gives the last word of the last line filed previously. Sometimes it gives the length of the add, as it does in this example from an AP TTS monitor.

```
    A096
        qyyyx
    Assassination Add 50

    ATHENS Assassination at-
tempt Lead A090 add:  capital.
    The bombs exploded in Athens
were described as home-made
devices filled with gasoline.
    The bomb that blew up near
the premier's car was pictured
as a more professional device,
a bundle of dynamite attached to
a plunger box hidden on the
rocky slope on the coastal side
of the road.

SF1103aed Aug. 13
```

The same technique is used for inserts. Since the wire service cannot show physically, on a proof, where an insert is to go, it must describe the spot clearly. The instructions include the last word of the paragraph that precedes the insert and the first word of the paragraph that follows. An insert on a UPI monitor looks like this:

```
035
     zzzyrwyd Caller 8-13 d
Insert in 020 after 8th pgh xxx
Marilyn.

      Police said relatives of Mrs.
Clark said she had worked
briefly as a secretary at Emory
University and had gone to
Florida with her daughter to
```

```
seek a job.  Mrs. Clark,
separated from her husband,
had registered with her daugh-
ter at a Miami hotel, officers
said.

Pickup 9th pgh:  While
                  —
```

New leads are filed on the teletype as a story develops. The basic or "budget" story begins with a "night lead," for morning newspapers, or a "day lead," for afternoon papers. New leads are slugged "first lead," "second lead," "third lead," and so on. Sometimes a new lead moves in takes. Typical slugs are then "first add fourth lead shooting," "second add fourth lead shooting," and the like. On important fast-breaking stories, the service supplements the new leads with "bulletins" and "flashes" that summarize developments.

A new lead on a regional AP wire for morning newspapers looks like this:

```
62
          yyxlbyl
                    h-47
                             jr30
Steel Bjt 4th NL  41

      PITTSBURGH AP - The
United Steelworkers Union, nar-
rowly rejecting demands for a
strike, approved a new, billion-
dollar labor contract Tuesday
night - largest in its 32-year
history.
     President I.W. Abel . . .
     Industry negotiators . . .
     Here is what the contract . . .
     The best previous steelworker
contract was the 47.3 cents an
hour won in 1964, during the last
negotiations.  Before that, also in
three-year pacts but backed up
by strikes, the union gained 45.7
cents in 1956 and 40 cents in
1959.
     Most of the, 7th graf 41
```

When a paragraph is killed and replaced by another, the new material is called a "sub." On a UPI TTS wire it looks like this:

```
043
      zzuvzyr talks 8-13 nw
Sub 038 3rd pgh bgng:  Tho

      Tho, the seventh-ranking
member of North Vietnam's
Politburo, arrived today after a
three-day stopover en route
from Hanoi.  He had spent a
good part of six weeks
discussing strategy with Ho Chi
Minh.
     He had no comment for
reporters at the airport except
to say his return to Paris "is
part of my normal work."

Pickup 4th pgh:  Diplomatic
```

—

Corrections are handled with similar logic. Here is a correction as it appeared on an AP TTS state wire:

```
V11
      ktk
            cs540aed 5c

CORRECTION
     NEW YORK - Farm Roundup
v9 in fourth graf, last line make
figure 3.6 per cent fixing gar-
ble.

The AP
```

—

Since the assembly instructions on wire copy are for the use of the desk, not the composing room, the copyreader deletes them. If he still has the story on his desk when the revisions are filed, he pastes the fresh material where it belongs. If he has sent the story to the composing room, he makes the changes on the proof, just as he would on a local story.

Printing Instructions

SINCE the editor, not the printer, determines the size, column width, and style of type to be used, the copyreader must send instructions on these matters to the composing room. He writes them in longhand, usually at the top of the copy, but when necessary in the margins or between lines. The amount of detail depends largely on how much variety the newspaper gets into its typography. The more variety, the more need for detailed instructions.

In the newsroom and in the composing room, size is described not in inches but in the printer's units of measure: the point, the pica, and the em.

The point is about 1/72 of an inch. There are 12 points in a pica, and therefore 6 picas in an inch. The em is really a measure of quantity, not distance, but in editorial practice the term usually means the same as pica.

Type is measured from top to bottom, in points. The width of a column or a line of type or a picture is usually expressed in picas. The term em, as a synonym for pica, is used most often for short horizontal measures—the depth of indentations, the length of dashes, and the like. The size of a story or picture measured from top to bottom (known as its depth) is usually expressed in picas, sometimes in inches.

Since the point is roughly 1/72 of an inch, a headline set in 72-point type measures roughly one inch from the top of the ascenders (the parts of the letters that are above the center body, like the stems of h and b) to the bottom of the descenders (like the stem of p and the loop of g).

The size of the slug, or base on which the letters stand, is also expressed in points. The slug does not take ink or touch the printing surface. It is strictly a platform, and when it extends beyond the extremes of the letters it provides white space on the page. An 8-point type on a 9-point slug, for example, produces a printed line with half a point of white space above and below it. If one slug is placed above another, there will be a point of white space between the lines. In the printing plant, an 8-point type on a 9-point slug is called "8 on 9."

Since there are six picas in an inch, an 11-pica column is just under two inches wide. For many years the standard column in an eight-column newspaper was 12 picas. In the last 30 years, however, the column has generally been narrowed to 10½ or 11 picas, and many newspapers, in adopting livelier modern dress, have made extensive use of odd measures, like 14 or 17 picas, that fall somewhere between the old standards for one-column and two-column widths.

(If you hear that a line is 14.3 picas wide, by the way, be on guard: the width is not 14 3/10 picas, but 14 picas, 3 points, or 14¼ picas.)

As has been noted, the newsman uses "em" as a synonym for pica in expressing short horizontal measurements. If he writes "indent 1 em left and right" (or "mutt-mutt"), the story will be indented one pica at each side. If he calls for a "3-em dash," he'll get a half-inch dash.

In some offices you'll also run into the en, which is half an em. It usually designates an indentation, and may be expressed as "nut left" (indent one en at the left), "nut right," or "nut-nut" (indent one en each side). Pretty silly, huh?

In addition to being told the size, the printer must be told the style of type to use. There are many different designs, called "families," each of which can be produced in different "faces": light (normal), bold (extra black), medium bold (in between), roman (upright), italic (slanted to the right), upper case (capitals), lower case (small letters), condensed (narrow letters), and extended (broad letters). The families are distinguished by differences in appearance and are often named for the designer: Bodoni, Caslon, and Baskerville, are commonly seen.

Because of differences in design, they serve different purposes. A paper may use Bodoni, Caslon, Futura, or Vogue for its headlines, Century or Corona or Ionic for body type, and Spartan for sports summaries, stock market quotations, and other tabular matter.

A paper normally relies on a single family for most of its body type, and in many offices the copyreader specifies type family only when something other than the basic type is desired. It is often assumed, also, that unless italic or bold face is specified the type will be set in light-face roman.

Thus, to order a story set to 1-column measure in light-face Corona roman, 8-point on a 9-point slug, capitals and lower case, you could write the instructions this way:

```
1-col 8/9 corona lite roman, clc
```

But if 1-column 8 on 9 Corona is your workhorse body type, it's more likely that you'll do it this way:

```
1-8 lite  or  1-8
```

Or you may just skip the instructions entirely, on the understanding that the usual body type will be used.

Any deviations from the normal, of course, demand detailed instructions, which can get pretty complex. To order 8-point light-face Century italics on a 10-point slug, caps and lower case, set to a width of 14.3 picas but indented one en on each side, you could write:

```
8/10 Century lite itals clc x 14.3 pi nut-nut
```

The newcomer to copyreading may find this incomprehensible, but he should not despair. No matter how complex the order seems, it is only telling the printer what kind of type and what measure he is to use. The translation is simple, if one knows the vocabulary.

The editor normally draws a line around the printing instructions. This helps the printer spot the orders and also tells him, in cases of doubt, that the enclosed words are for his information and should not be set in type as part of the story.

As already indicated, the editor uses many abbreviations and phonetic spellings. The most frequently used are "col," "pt," "em," "pi," "caps," "lc" (for lower case), "clc" (for caps and lower case), "lite," "bld," "ro" (for roman), "itals," "indent," "aget" (for agate, or 5½-point type), "flush left" (to the extreme left of the column), "flush right," and "centered."

Instructions to indent, center, or set flush left or flush right can be buttressed with symbols, or the symbols can stand alone:

```
and that government of the
people, by the people, for the
people shall not perish from
the earth.
```

(indent left)

```
and that government of the
people, by the people, for the
people shall not perish from
the earth.
```

(indent right)

```
and that government of the
people, by the people, for the
people shall not perish from
the earth.
```

(indent both sides)

```
Lincoln's Address
```

(center)

```
Lincoln's Address
```

(flush left)

```
Lincoln's Address
```

(flush right)

The Latin word "stet" means "let it stand"; it tells the printer that regardless of penciled deletions or changes (which often can't be erased completely) the copy should be set as originally typewritten. Or, if "stet" appears on proof, it means that the type should be left as it is. It's usually a sign that an editor or proofreader has had second thoughts about a change, but it's also a convenient symbol for "leave it alone" when a printer or proofreader sends copy back to the newsroom with a question.

The letters "cq," circled, are sometimes used to head off such time-consuming questions. When a spelling or a fact is so unusual or improbable that it's almost certain to be questioned (the name John Smiht, for example, or a blue ribbon awarded to a "milking shorthorn bull"), the reporter or editor who has checked it and knows that it is correct may insert "cq" as notice that he is aware of the oddness and certifies its accuracy. And he'd better be right.

Various devices are used for typographical effect. One of the most common is the subhead, a line of prominent type that is used to break up a mass of body type and serves as a heading for the material under it. It can be set in many ways: the same size as the body type, but bold face and centered; the size of the body type, but bold face and flush left; or larger than the body type, centered or flush left, roman or italics, light face or bold face, all capitals, or capitals and lower case.

All offices prescribe the style of subheads, and most have rules, related to the length of the story, about when to use them. The copyreader normally writes the subhead on the copy, cutting the copy apart and pasting in blank paper if necessary to provide space, and then writes in the printing instructions according to his office's procedure. Here are some of the ways the subhead can look:

] Three - Point Plan [(8 pt bld clc)

] Three - Point Plan [(sh) (for subhead)

[Three - Point Plan (10 pt lite itals subhead flush left)

Three - Point Plan (10 pt bld clc centered)

The copyreader must also put printing instructions on by-lines. Style varies, but this is typical of how a by-line would appear:

] By MARY SCANLON [(8 pt bld caps)

] Dispatch Staff Writer [(aget lite clc)

There are other specialized words, abbreviations, and symbols of more limited application. "Init," usually with the type size added (as in "24-pt init"), means to start a paragraph with one letter set in larger type than the rest, and usually in bold face. A "lead-in" can be a couple of words set in bold face at the start of a paragraph. A "bullet' is an oversized period used to call attention to a paragraph, or to each of the items in a list. Stars and asterisks can serve a similar purpose. In one newsroom a "dingbat" may be a generic term covering bullets, stars, asterisks, and similar devices, while in another it may be a specific decoration, like a curlycue or "lazy S," used to fill white space. The copyreader needn't worry about being familiar with all of them. He quickly learns the ones used in his office.

Leads

DURING a summer of urban rioting, a reporter wrote this lead for a story about an investigating commission:

> In Detroit, police raid an after-hours Negro drinking club. In Newark, they arrest a Negro cab driver for tailgating. In Watts, they stop two Negro youths in a car and charge the driver with speeding.
>
> Similar events take place—and pass unnoticed—in American cities nearly every night of the week. Who could have known that this time a crowd would collect, that its emotions would turn against the police, and that a city would shortly be engulfed in a cyclone of lawlessness and equally massive suppression?
>
> What can be done after such commonplace incidents occur to insure that a bloody and costly riot will not erupt in their wake? If violence flares, can it be tamped down before a civil disturbance spins itself into a vortex of looting, arson and sniping?

The copyreader liked the approach but felt that the lead was overwritten. He was bothered by the mixture of metaphors, the question technique, and the heavy emphasis on the incidents—by then well known—that had precipitated the riots. So he rewrote the lead this way:

> Police in American cities make traffic arrests and raid drinking places every night and nothing happens. But then there is a night in

```
Watts and a youth is arrested for speeding.  There
is a night in Newark and a cab driver is arrested
for tailgating.  There is a night in Detroit and
an after-hours club is shut down.
     There are other nights in other cities, and
suddenly America is wondering what it takes to
prevent the eruption of violence after common-
place events, and what it takes to stop the vio-
lence once it has erupted.
```

The rewrite says the same thing as the original, and preserves the tone by using much of the same language. It doesn't rob the reporter of his style, but it does make the style a little less flamboyant. Through minor changes in organization and word choice, it shifts the emphasis from the old riot news to the current dilemma of the nation. By changing questions to statements of fact, it eliminates the undertone of plaintive uncertainty.

The function of the copy desk is to edit, not rewrite, and the copyreader should resist the impulse to do the reporter's work over. Nevertheless, the lead sometimes requires the extra help that only a rewrite can provide. The lead can be the most important single element in the story, and the copyreader should examine it closely for content and technique.

He should ask himself some questions. Is it the "right" lead? Does it deal with an important element of the story? Does it get right to the point? Is it interesting? Is it clear? Is it accurate? Is it consistent with the rest of the story? Does it include essential elements of time and place?

If the copyreader finds he can't summarize the story neatly for a headline, or has to go to the ninth paragraph for headline material, he knows there is something wrong. Usually, however, he can spot a bad lead before he writes the head. The lead may be a sweeping generality. It may be a drab, "ho-hum" scene setter. It may be incomplete, or ambiguous, or complex, or cluttered with trivia, or trite, or too tricky.

No copyreader would pass stories that began like these:

```
     Jack Nicklaus and Bob Murphy played
golf yesterday.

     The President spoke to Congress yes-
terday on the topic of "Taxes."

     The United States held a presidential
election yesterday.
```

Yet similar, no-account, say-nothing leads do get by, particularly in stories about speeches, meetings, and surveys. Here are three examples:

Vice President Hubert H. Humphrey, addressing students and faculty yesterday in the University Theater, answered questions from a panel of student body representatives.

In a meeting of the Committee for Responsible Action held last night in the Arts College building, several issues were discussed, two of which stood out.

In interviews during the past week, several Black and Indian students gave their opinions of the racial situation in the city and on campus.

The writers of those leads forgot to try to interest the reader. The Humphrey story could have started this way:

Vice President Hubert H. Humphrey told a University audience yesterday that a military settlement of the war in Vietnam is not possible.

The meeting story this way:

The Committee for Responsible Action will stage a march protesting the war in Vietnam regardless of whether it receives a city parade permit, its chairman said last night.

And the interview story this way:

Indian and Black students are divided in their opinion of the severity of the discrimination problem in town and on campus, a spot check shows.

A lead should do more than announce the subject of a story, or the topic of the speech the story covers. This one is weak:

Byron Eshelman, prison chaplain at San Quentin for 16 years, spoke on the paradox of prison life, "Punishment vs. Rehabilitation," last night.

All this lead does is identify the speaker. The title of his talk adds little; for, if the story reports what Mr. Eshelman said, his topic should be apparent.

Here is another variety of deadly "topic" lead:

> "Responsive and Responsible" state government were the main points of an address by State Sen. LeRoy Anderson, a candidate for the Democratic nomination for governor, on the campus yesterday.

This lead doesn't give the speech title, but it's no more informative than the Eshelman lead. The copyreader should watch for expressions like "were the main points," "was the subject of," "will be the topic of," "spoke on the subject," and "was among the items discussed by." They warn that the writer is reporting topics, not what the speaker said.

It's easier to diagnose the "topic" lead than to treat it. The copyreader can usually do one of three things: (1) send the story back to the reporter, (2) take meaningful material from later paragraphs and edit it into the lead, or (3) rewrite the lead and edit the rest of the story to conform.

The second course is usually the best because it is fast and relatively safe. The Eshelman and Anderson stories could have been edited this way:

> Byron Eshelman, prison chaplain at San Quentin for 16 years, said ~~spoke on the paradox of prison life, "Punishment vs. Rehabilitation,"~~ last night, that
>
> "A median must be found between the lash and the carrot," ~~Mr. Eshelman said.~~ if American prisons are to
>
> ~~He warned that unless reforms are effected, American prisons will continue indefinitely to harden rather than~~ ameliorate rather than continue to harden ~~orate~~ the criminal characteristics of their inmates.

~~"Responsive and Responsible" state government were the main points of an address by~~ State Sen. LeRoy Anderson, a candidate for the Democratic nomination for governor, said on the campus yesterday, that

~~The public is generally "frustrated and unhappy," Anderson said, because~~ under the state's system of government by appointed boards and commissions, the state government is neither responsible to the voters nor responsive to their will.

If the construction of the story precludes this type of editing, the copyreader should rewrite. Here are some "blah" leads, followed by possible rewrites:

Original

A special meeting of the Board of Trustees of the InterBel Telephone Cooperative, Inc., was held at the office of the cooperative in Eureka yesterday.

Rewrite

The Board of Trustees of InterBel Telephone Cooperative voted yesterday to apply for a loan of $62,000 from the Rural Electrification Administration to extend service to 97 new subscribers.

* * *

Original

```
    The July 1 issue of Business Week
magazine gives pointers about the need
for early driver training for teen-agers.
```

Rewrite

```
    Teen-age drivers will be better drivers
if their instructors take the trouble to
scare them a little, according to an article
in the July 1 issue of Business Week magazine.
```

* * *

Original

```
    John and Larry Mohar have modernized
the buildings and equipment on their farm,
18 miles north of Harlem on the Turner Road.
```

Rewrite

```
    It's a luxurious world for the 600
pigs at the Mohar farm, 18 miles north
of Harlem on the Turner Road.
```

The original leads just cited are weak mainly because they are more like printed programs than accounts of the game. The sports writer who reports that Missouri beat Nebraska doesn't have to say that Missouri *played* Nebraska. Similarly, the writer who reports on a speech or a meeting or a construction project doesn't have to say that the speakers spoke, the meeters met, or the builders built.

The copyreader must watch for the lead that is too general. Every story is unique in some way. Even if it's only about a Ladies' Aid meeting or a fender bender or the arrival of fall, it has an element of time, place, cause, or cast of characters which makes it unprecedented and unduplicatable. The lead should recognize that.

An interview with a professor of forensic medicine began this way: "One doesn't meet a physician-lawyer every day." Nope, one doesn't. Nor does one meet a bartender-barber every day. But both facts are irrelevant to the circumstances that make a physician-lawyer or a bartender-barber worth writing about.

A story about a nursing specialist began this way: "A special kind of nurse exists today." An unchallengeable fact. But it's probably also true that some kind of nurse has been a "special kind" since the days of Miss Nightingale. And it's also true that special kinds of teachers, clergymen, mechanics, engineers, waiters, accountants, store clerks, and parachutists exist today. The lead overlooks the uniqueness of the story.

So does this lead, from a story about the male supervisor of a women's dormitory: " 'I do it to eat,' the burly history major said, when asked why he chose to be a babysitter for 287 girls." The same basic motivation could probably be found in a shepherd, a real estate broker, a burglar, or a cab driver.

There is a comparable fault in this lead: "Medical illustrators deal with the unusual." But so do sideshow barkers, deep-sea divers, and astronauts.

Another kind of general lead is the broad statement that comments on life in general or the world around us, or guesses, without documentation, about the general application of the facts developed for a specific story.

Here's how one reporter tried to brighten a routine advance notice about a club meeting: "With spring comes many new things, such as the installation of officers of the Overlook Community Club." Since the story was about the club meeting and had nothing to do with the other new things of spring, a straightforward lead about the installation would have been better.

Here's a lead on a story dealing with the functions of a computer in a registrar's office: "Getting grade reports ready for over 30,000 students at the end of each quarter is a great task." Doubtless. But the sentence doesn't tell the reader anything about the problem or its solution.

A story on another problem of the multiversity began like this: "Many of us are unaware of the complex operations that go on around us each day." An unarguable statement, but so what?

Here's a lead on a fashion story: "Every season of the year brings forth an array of new and exciting styles and colors to delight women who love clothes." This may or may not be true, but either way it tells the reader nothing about the new and exciting styles and colors that are going to delight her *this* season—and that's what this story was about.

Beware of the lead that goes beyond the facts. In a story about student demands for administrative reforms, one campus newspaper led with this: "Almost every college administration reports increasing pressure from students to relax rules and regulations." The copyreader might have wondered how many hundreds of college administrations the reporter had checked as a basis for this startlingly broad statement.

Editing such poor leads isn't always as tough as it looks. The reporter who starts with a meaningless or inappropriate generality often gets down to business in the second paragraph, and when he does the copyreader can edit the later material into the lead like this:

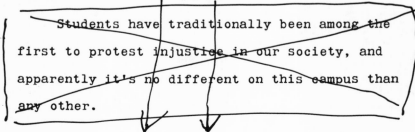

~~Students have traditionally been among the first to protest injustice in our society, and apparently it's no different on this campus than any other.~~

~~Yesterday,~~ About 100 students pitched tents on the Oval yesterday and began a 48-hour fast as a gesture of sympthy towards the Rev. Abernathy and his Poor People's Campaign in Washington, D.C.

A lead can be specific, yet off target. A story of a meeting began this way:

> To be considered a good teacher in the educational system of the United States today, according to Edward Reinholtz, chairman of the art department, a person must teach "discipline" and "the right way."

The story quoted Reinholtz as saying that art teachers, for self-protection, force their students into the "discipline" and "right way" referred to. The copyreader felt that the lead's meaning depended too heavily on the explanation that followed. He rewrote like this:

> American art teachers are strangling creativity in their students, Edward Reinholtz, chairman of the art department, told the Student Education Association last night.
>
> Reinholtz said the teacher knows that he must teach "discipline" and "the right way" if he is to win the approval of his superiors.

The rewrite is more specific and more understandable than the original.

A story on a speech by a foreign correspondent began this way:

> The Chinese food shortage is one of the most pressing problems of today, Pulitzer Prize-winning Harrison Salisbury told an audience of more than 1,000 persons in the University Theater last night. Mr. Salisbury said that unless China can solve its food problem through negotiation and trade agreements, she will "explode with physical force and attack the countries that have the food it needs."

The copyreader felt that the first sentence was pretty much wasted and that the "true lead" was in the second sentence. He modified the paragraph this way:

> Unless China can solve its food problem through negotiations and trade agreements, it will "explode with physical force and attack the countries that have the food its needs," Harrison Salisbury of the New York Times said in the University Theater last night.

Another story on the same speech began like this:

> Harrison Salisbury, assistant managing editor of the New York Times, told students and faculty last night that there is something paranoid in the thinking of Peking.

Like the other lead on the speech, this one stops short of making a point. Here's what an editor did with it:

> Harrison Salisbury, assistant managing
>
> editor of the New York Times, told students
>
> and faculty last night that ~~there is some-~~ Peking's
>
> ~~thing~~ " paranoid ~~in the~~ " thinking ~~of Peking.~~
>
> could cause China to start a nuclear war.

Here's a lead on a story about a conflict between citizens and government:

> A major conflict has arisen during the past year between holders of special use permits of government property and Forest Service and federal officials, due to increased and hastening revocation of the permits.

The copyreader was bothered by the first clause because it said so little ("major conflicts" are arising all the time). He felt that the true lead was buried in the "due to" clause, and rewrote like this:

```
        The shores of Seeley Lake have become a
    battleground in the federal government's
    campaign to repossess lands which for many
    years have been leased to private citizens.
```

Immediacy is important to news writing, and whenever possible the copyreader should update the lead in a story that is based on "old" news. Updating is a bigger problem on weeklies than it is on dailies, and the copyreader should not strain to make it appear that his weekly or monthly publication is in fact a daily. But if he is handling a story about a week-old meeting, and it mentions an activity that is planned for the future, he should consider whether the story would have greater impact if he based the lead on the future event or on the meeting report.

In addition to checking content, the copyreader must read the lead for all the writing problems that may afflict the story as a whole, plus a few others. The reporter schooled in the "Five Ws" may write a lead that is so detailed that it's incomprehensible. The reporter seeking a bright approach may get so tricky that he misleads or makes no sense. The reporter who likes direct quotations may lead with a windy quotation when a paraphrase would have more punch. The reporter who just can't think of a good lead may use the hackneyed question technique.

There's no real trick to writing a lead that answers all the basic "W" questions. Anyone who knows grammar can do it. But rarely should the hurried reporter try, because the old-fashioned lead that tells the whole story in a single sentence, and is usually too overloaded with detail to be clear, is often what he comes up with. For example:

```
        James Brown, 20, a junior in architecture,
    suffered bruises of the chest and arms and
    Richard Fangbeetle, 23, a graduate student
    in zoology, suffered a fractured wrist and
    cuts of the head at 4:30 p.m. yesterday when
    a car being driven west on Pelican Street
    by Brown, with Fangbeetle as a passenger,
    was in collision with a delivery truck driven
    north on Eulalia Street by John Hemlock, 38,
    of 322 Spruce Street, and were admitted to
    City Hospital, where Brown was reported in
    good condition and Fangbeetle in fair con-
    dition just before midnight.
```

That is a made-up example, but it's not much harder to wade through than this one, which is real:

```
     Using chalk and a courtroom blackboard
to go over his calculations, Highway Patrolman
Harvey Hetrick, under cross-examination,
Tuesday maintained that John Patterson was
"driving at a speed in excess of 90 miles an
hour" when his car crashed into the station
wagon driven by Mrs. Richard McGrew, killing
the driver and five of her children.
```

Or this one, also real:

```
     A request for nearly $185,000 will be
submitted to the Office of Economic Oppor-
tunity for operating costs for the Missoula
Head Start and Day Care programs and the
programs in Alberton and St. Regis, the
board of directors of the Missoula-Mineral
Human Resources, Inc., decided Friday.
```

The copyreader should trim such leads, taking care to restore the deleted material further down in the story. He could edit these this way:

~~Using chalk and a courtroom blackboard~~
~~to go over his calculations,~~ Highway Patrolman
Harvey Hetrick, testified ~~under cross-examination,~~
Tuesday ~~maintained~~ that John Patterson was
~~"driving at a speed in excess of~~ going more than 90 miles an

> hour when his car crashed into the station wagon ~~driven by~~ of Mrs. Richard McGrew, killing ~~the driver~~ her and five of her children.

> ~~A request for~~ Nearly $185,000 will be ~~submitted to the Office of Economic Oppor-~~ requested ~~tunity for operating costs~~ for the ~~Missoula~~ Head Start and Day Care programs ~~and the programs in~~ in Missoula, Alberton and St. Regis, the board of directors of the Missoula-Mineral Human Resources, Inc., decided Friday.

But remember that a complex lead must not be simplified at the expense of essential information.

A lead written in the past tense must include a time factor. In most stories, some indication of *where* is also necessary. But the past tense lead that doesn't say *when* leaves the reader waiting for the other shoe to drop. Witness these leads, from which the time element has been deleted:

> NEW YORK — Dr. Grayson Kirk, a target in the student revolt at Columbia University last spring, retired as president of the University.

> Service units arrived at the O'Hare Air Force Base and at the Glenview Naval Air Station to prepare for the transportation and care of 7,500 federal troops if they are needed in Chicago during the Democratic National Convention next week.

> The city, along with the eastern two-thirds of the nation, struggled through another day of heat and humidity.

Each of those leads seems to shout one question: "When?"

In most cases, the future tense lead also demands a time element. Leads in the present and present perfect tenses can normally get along without it, however, as in these examples:

> SIM I, the USC School of Medicine's imitation human patient developed at a cost of $275,000, is not being used for research because of a lack of money.
>
> CHICAGO (UPI) — Science calls the ailment hyperhiddrosis. In plain terms, it is excessive perspiring, often annoying but not harmful.

While the *where* element is sometimes implicit in the lead ("Congress is not expected to act this year on a bill to ban cigarette advertising on radio and television" or "Most Americans oppose the legalization of marijuana, an opinion survey has shown"), the hard-news story usually requires it. This lead doesn't tell much:

> Two deputy sheriffs braved smoke and flames early Thursday to rescue two men lying unconscious in their apartment.

But with the place element added it has meaning:

> Two deputy sheriffs braved smoke and flames early Thursday to rescue two men lying unconscious in their burning apartment in La Mirada.

Although the copyreader should be prepared to trim the long, rambling lead, he should remember that brevity in itself does not guarantee clarity. Short sentences can be ambiguous, particularly in speech and meeting stories that include references to time and place. For example:

> Prof. Jack Birkelbach said expulsions and suspensions are not the answer to student misconduct last night at a Student Senate meeting in the Student Union.

The copyreader could eliminate the ambiguity in several ways:

~~Prof. Jack Birkelbach said~~

Expulsions and suspensions are not

the answer to student misconduct,

Prof. Jack Birkelbach said

last night at a Student Senate

meeting in the Student Union.

last night that

Prof. Jack Birkelbach said

expulsions and suspensions are not

the answer to student misconduct.

He spoke

~~last night~~ at a Student Senate

meeting in the Student Union.

~~Prof. Jack Birkelbach said~~

Expulsions and suspensions are not

the answer to student misconduct,

Prof. Jack Birkelbach told the

~~last night at a~~ Student Senate

at a last night.

meeting in the Student Union

A construction can be grammatical but still ambiguous. Witness this lead on a story about a coed with an ambition to be a funeral director:

> Marguerite DeNardo decided to become an undertaker because she likes working with people.

Incompleteness or misplaced emphasis can produce puzzlers like this:

> A presentence report was ordered Monday in the case of a 24-year-old man said to have helped the Spokane County sheriff's department recover $8,500 worth of stolen articles.

In this case the story contained all the information the copyreader needed in order to make this alteration:

> A presentence report was ordered Monday in the case of a 24-year-old confessed thief who reportedly ~~man said to have~~ helped the Spokane County sheriff's department recover $8,500 worth of stolen articles.

Complex subject matter can be made incomprehensible by a complex lead. A reporter who lacks the confidence or skill to translate legal, scientific, or sociological language into layman's terms may ensure accuracy by making his story follow the procedural pattern of the event he is covering. There is safety in this course, but clarity may require that he cut away the procedural details and expose the meaning. A couple of examples:

> OTTAWA — An opposition move to delete from a government bill a proposal to exempt American lake vessels from compulsory pilotage dues on the Canadian section of the St. Lawrence Seaway between Cornwell and Montreal was defeated today.

> WASHINGTON — The Supreme Court yesterday reversed a decision of the First U.S. Circuit Court of Appeals in which the controversial 1966 law that

```
makes it a federal crime to burn or
otherwise destroy or mutilate a draft
card was declared unconstitutional as
an infringement of the right of free
speech.
```

The first of these mind breakers means that the government won support for its plan to exempt American vessels from compulsory pilotage dues on a section of the seaway. The second means that the United States Supreme Court upheld the law making it a crime to mutilate a draft card.

Short leads as well as long ones may be wordy. Here's a 19-word lead that could be cut to 15 words with no loss of content:

```
        Two separate highway accidents yesterday

claimed the lives of an Easton man and two

teen-age girls from Binghamton, N.Y.
```

The copyreader should first knock out "separate." It adds nothing. Then he should change the pompous phrase "claimed the lives of" to "killed." Now he has this:

Two ~~separate~~ highway accidents yesterday

~~claimed the lives of~~ killed an Easton man and two

teen-age girls from Binghamton, N.Y.

Now that the fat has been trimmed off, it's clear that the *where* element is missing. The copyreader should write it in.

Some leads are too tricky for their own good. While the writer should try to be different, he should make sure that what he writes is relevant and true. Here's a nice bright lead:

```
    A possum bit a man in a bar and
walked all the way to police head-
quarters to give itself up.
```

Unfortunately, it's a fake. The rest of the story makes it clear that there were *two* possums, one in the bar and one at the police station.

The one-word lead usually boomerangs, too:

> Polarity. That was the point made over and over by Prof. Thomas McQueen in his lecture on race relations last night.

Aside from the fact that "polarity" is hardly a "point," this paragraph gives no information other than the name of the speaker and his topic. A straightforward lead like this would be better:

> America's views on race relations are being polarized, and there are few effective leaders who stand between the extremes, Prof. Thomas McQueen said last night.

Analogies can be effective in making complex subjects or unusual situations or high numbers understandable, but they should be reasonable analogies. Sometimes a writer reaches too far and comes up with a silly one, like this:

> If you ever budgeted to spend $9.4 million and then found only $800,000 in the federal till, you have an idea of the State Highway Department's present situation.

It's unlikely that many newspaper readers ever have had the problem, so the analogy is phony. To demonstrate the weakness of the approach, let's rewrite two other leads from the same front page:

> If you have ever been a college president who ordered the removal of four hippie newspapers from the college bookstore and then had to explain the action to the Student Senate, you will have some understanding of Leon H. Johnson's problem.
>
> If you have ever owned a horse that won the Kentucky Derby and then had it disqualified because of the presence of painkiller in its system, you will have an idea of how Peter Fuller feels today.

Allied to the phony analogy lead is the phony question lead. The question is usually a device for backing into a story:

```
        Have you ever wondered why the library
    closes at 11 p.m. on Saturday, instead of at
    midnight as on other days of the week?
```

This lead is weak because the reader's state of mind is irrelevant. The story is not about the reader's question, but about the librarian's answer.

The question lead is appropriate when the story deals with a matter that has actually been of widespread speculation. There is no intrinsic fault in this approach:

```
        Did Lee Harvey Oswald act alone, as
    the Warren Commission believed, or was
    he just one member of a ring of con-
    spirators?  Another in a growing list of
    authors thinks that he has found the answer.
```

Such situations are rare, however. The question lead usually leaves the reader cold. It gives him no information, it makes the writer seem uncertain rather than confident, and it can deaden the interest of the reader to whom the question has never occurred. Here's one that can't possibly touch more than 50 percent of the readership:

```
        Have you ever wondered how it feels
    to be elected Homecoming Queen?
```

Here's one that depends for meaning on the questioner's inflection, a hard thing to convey in print:

```
        Is one man living with 270
    women to be pitied or envied?
```

Read one way, the question demands an answer of either "pitied" or "envied." But, read another way, the answer must be "yes" or "no."

Like the question lead, the lead that consists of a direct quotation, with only attribution added, usually lacks force and fails to give the story direction. A direct quotation short enough to get the story moving may not say enough to make the speaker's point clear. On the other hand, people are windier when they talk than when they write, and as a result the direct quote lead is usually wordy and roundabout.

Suppose a governor gives a speech in which he says: "In view of these circumstances, I will in coming weeks propose that the General Assembly enact appropriate legislation to approximately double the benefits now paid to humane societies under the Veticare program." The reporter covering the speech might lead this way:

> "I will in coming weeks propose that the General Assembly enact appropriate legislation to approximately double the benefits now paid to humane societies under the Veticare program," Gov. Hess said yesterday.

On the other hand, he might lead with this:

> Gov. Hess proposed yesterday that the state double the benefits paid to humane societies under the Veticare program.

The second lead is more forceful because it aims the story directly at Gov. Hess' main point instead of letting it ramble about. The copyreader must remember that a speech is not a news story, any more than a news story is a speech.

This principle is sound whether the speech has been made by the President of the United States, the Tail Twister of the Lions Club, the business manager of the International Ladies Garment Workers Union, or a professional after-dinner speaker. Consider this accurate but say-nothing lead:

> "Our military cause is totally irrelevant to what is going on in Vietnam," Robert Eaton, captain of the Quaker yacht Phoenix, said last night.

Except for those who heard the speech, few readers would know from that lead what Eaton was driving at. They shouldn't have to read the whole story to find out. The lead should be understandable in itself.

If a direct or indirect quotation is used in the lead, it should be linked grammatically to the speaker. It should not be set down by itself and then be explained in a later sentence, as it is in this hypothetical example:

```
     "I am no appeaser."

     So said Harry P. Thrust, presi-

dent of Thrust & Parry, Inc., in

explaining why the sword manufacturing

concern had rejected a union demand

for greater safety precautions in the

company's quality control testing

program.
```

Edited, without changing the quotation, this lead could read:

```
     "I am no appeaser,"

     So said Harry P. Thrust, presi-
                              (said yesterday)
dent of Thrust & Parry, Inc., in

explaining why the sword manufacturing

concern had rejected a union demand

for greater safety precautions in the

company's quality control testing

program.
```

The copyreader should also check the lead for inappropriate language. Here's an example from the real world:

```
     President Johnson's announcement Sunday
night that he would not seek re-election
stunned Oregon's political leaders into ex-
pressions of surprise, disappointment, praise
and bitterness.
```

The word "stun" means to daze or paralyze or shock into unconsciousness. Since it's hard to imagine anyone being paralyzed into action, the copyreader should have changed the word to "shocked" or "aroused" or "spurred" or some more believable verb.

A lead that backs into a story with a subordinate clause or phrase is generally less forceful than the one that goes straight to the point with a standard subject-verb-object construction. The introductory phrases in these leads are distracting:

> During the annual recognition program of the College of Agriculture and Home Economics last night, more than 600 students and faculty were honored for service to the University and the College.

> At the Board of Trustees meeting yesterday, Richard C. Drorbaugh of Madison was elected president.

> Acting on the advice of the Faculty Advisory Committee (FAC), the Council on Academic Affairs (CAA) and the Commission on University Development (CUD), President Henry B. Trawler yesterday announced he is recommending the appointment of Dr. Hulburd T. Swillinger as vice president for academic affairs and provost of the university.

The lead should deliver the news, and it should highlight a point that is to be a major one in the development of the story. Some leads collapse because, while lively and interesting, they promise things that the story doesn't provide. A case in point, from a campus newspaper:

> "Your daddy's a jailbird. Your daddy's a nigger-lover." These verbal harassments have been directed toward Prof. David McMurtrie's children ever since their father became prominent in the Black Power movement.

Despite the direct quotation, that is a powerful lead. The reader will want to know who these youngsters are, where they are being harassed, who is doing the harassing, how the children are reacting to it, how their parents feel about it, whether the children have friends who defend them, and what their teachers are doing to protect them.

But in this story the reader never found out. There was no further reference to the children. So the lead was phony.

That is not to say that a lead should not take a fresh approach. It certainly should, and the copyreader should have enough sense to leave a good one alone.

A *New York Times* reporter, on a routine weather assignment story, wrote this:

```
        After a week of tears, April bowed
    out yesterday in a glow of golden laughter.
```

The copyreader didn't touch it. He was right.

Story Organization

POOR story organization is hard to repair. Major changes can require complete rewriting, and there is seldom time for that. Lesser changes can sometimes do a lot of good, however, and if he has time to, the copyreader should uncover the buried lead, bring out the local angle in a wire story, provide transitions where needed, and switch blocks of material about for greater clarity and interest.

Every story should be organized with some regard for the importance and relationship of events. If chronology is important, the writer should provide it. But the sequence of events is often of little significance. The news in a speech may be near the end, as it was when President Johnson announced that he would not seek reelection in 1968. The news in a meeting can come at the end, in the middle, or at the start. A football game may be decided on the opening kickoff or on the last play, or even after it's over if a player is disqualified or if an official has made a monstrous mistake.

Regardless of chronology, it is the reporter's job to be selective, to pick out the high spots and emphasize them. If he doesn't, the copyreader should help. These two passages show how deadly the chronological approach can be:

> Joe Wagner, president of the Forestry Club, opened the meeting by asking for the reading of the minutes of the last meeting and the treasury report.

> James Parker, the committee's chairman, began the informal meeting of about 50 people by requesting a discussion of the parking lot cleanup campaign, which the committee is undertaking.

Barring some dramatic response to Wagner and Parker, the paragraphs should be edited like this:

> Joe Wagner, ~~president of the Forestry Club,~~ opened the meeting ~~by asking for~~ the reading of the minutes ~~of~~ the last meeting and ~~the treasury report~~.
>
> James Parker, the committee's chairman, began the ~~informal~~ meeting of about ~~50~~ people by requesting a discussion ~~of the~~ parking lot cleanup campaign, which the committee is undertaking.

The copyreader should rescue the buried lead, uncover the hidden local angle in wire copy. Here the lead is buried under a landslide of words:

> More than one and a half billion board feet of timber is harvested in the 16 national forests of the Northern Region each year. Timber prices are established in competitive bidding.
>
> As the timber is hauled out of the national forests, the logs are scaled (measured) to determine the actual volume of timber the purchaser has harvested. In the past every log was scaled on National Forest timber sales. If such complete harvesting were practiced today, it would cost about $550,000 a year in the national forests of eastern Washington, northern Idaho, South Dakota and western Montana.
>
> Today more than 60 per cent of the Northern Region's timber harvest is sample scaled to determine timber volumes.
>
> "This new technique is saving the woods products industry time, manpower and money," Kenneth R. Larson, Northern Regions scaler for the Forest Service, says. "While there are many timber harvesters who feel that a scaling stick has to be put on every log, more and more are finding sample scaling efficient and economical."

The copyreader who has waded through this may not be sure what the story is really about. He can try out the possibilities:

That 1.5 billion board feet of timber are harvested annually in the Northern Region? That's what the lead says.

That logs hauled out of the national forests are measured to determine timber volume, or that in the past every log was scaled, or that it would cost half a million dollars a year to scale every log if complete scaling were practiced today? That's what the second paragraph says.

That the modern practice is to sample scale? That's what the third paragraph says.

That, according to Mr. Larson, sample scaling is an improvement? That's way down in the fourth paragraph, but it's the real lead. The copyreader might write it like this:

> A new technique for measuring logs taken from forests is reported to be saving the wood products industry time, manpower and money.

All that remains is to paste the original story onto the new lead and edit Larson's comment to eliminate repetition. The changes would take seconds.

Similar handling is desirable when a wire service story has a local angle that is buried way, way down.

When a graduate of the University of Montana figured in an AP sports story, the community newspaper carried this headline:

> Magnuson Cut
> By Washington

That properly gets at the item of local interest. But here is how the story went:

> CARLISLE, Pa. (AP) — The Washington Redskins will test Bobby Mitchell's return as a fulltime running back in pro football's exhibition opener Thursday night against Houston.
>
> Coach Otto Graham named Mitchell, the former Cleveland speedster who now ranks as the NFL's No. 1 active pass receiver, to start at halfback, with tight end Jerry Smith shifting to flanker as his replacement.

> Jim Ninowski will start at quarterback in place of Sonny Jurgensen, still recovering from an elbow operation.
>
> The Redskins cut six more players from their training squad Tuesday, including veteran tackle John Kelly, injured linebacker Jim Steffen, and four rookies, running back Bryan Magnuson of Montana, defensive back Alden Reeves of Louisiana Tech, flanker Frank Sumpter of Maryland State and linebacker John Stipech of Utah.

Lack of time or management's orders to avoid resetting TTS copy can hamper the copyreader, but he should do his best to revamp such material in order to place the emphasis where it belongs and to make story and headline harmonize. In this case the change would not have to be extensive. The lead could be rewritten this way:

> CARLISLE, Pa. (AP) — Bryan Magnuson, a running back from Montana, was cut from the Washington roster Tuesday as the Redskins prepared to test Bobby Mitchell as a fulltime running back in pro football's exhibition opener Thursday night in Houston.

The next two paragraphs could stand unchanged, while the last would require the deletion of the reference to Magnuson.

Poor organization is more noticeable in the lead than elsewhere, but a solid lead is no guarantee that the rest of the story will not bog down. The entire story should emphasize action, not background or procedure.

Here is a story that is tedious because of misplaced emphasis:

> A change in the salaries paid to officers of Associated University Students was proposed by Steve Brown, AUS vice president, at Planning Board yesterday.
>
> Brown proposed an amendment to the AUS

Constitution which would establish a pay scale of $60 per month for nine months for the president, and $45 per month for nine months for the vice president, business manager and secretary each. Under the present system, the officers receive tuition scholarships.

Tuition scholarships are of unequal value, Brown said. Out-of-state tuition is $200 more per quarter than in-state tuition. For this reason the vice president last year, who was from out of state, was paid more than the president, who was from in state.

The amendment would also help stabilize the AUS budget, Brown said. Under the present system the variation in salaries makes it difficult to budget prior to election of officers.

The amendment would not be effective until the 1969-70 fiscal year, because next year's budget has already been approved, Brown said.

Brown also proposed an amendment that

would give Central Board the power, upon the recommendation of the vice president, "to dismiss by a two-thirds vote any commissioner who does not comply with the responsibilities accorded him by the vice president and the Constitution."

At present the vice president, who is in charge of the commissioners, has no control over them, Brown said. He told the board that it was difficult to get most commissioners to make their quarterly reports or to follow regulations.

One board member suggested that the power to recommend impeachment be widened to include all Central Board members, so the power could not be abused by one man.

Discussion of both amendments was tabled until next week.

This is a bad story because it doesn't get at the action. The lead deals with the proposal, not with its disposition, and is too general to get the story moving. A newspaper reader would go out of his mind if the typical lead read "The President proposed a change in the tax structure yesterday" or "The President commented yesterday on Sen. Dugan's proposal that the United States declare war on Iceland."

The principle is sound at the level of campus politics, too. The copyreader could have reorganized the story this way:

~~A change in the salaries paid to officers~~

~~of Associated University Students was proposed~~

proposed to

~~by~~ Steve Brown, AUS vice president, ~~at~~ Planning

Board yesterday, that

~~Brown proposed an amendment to~~ the AUS

be amended to salaries

Constitution ~~which would~~ establish ~~a pay scale~~

a

of $60 ~~per~~ month ~~for nine months~~ for the presi-

a each

dent, and $45 ~~per~~ month ~~for nine months~~ for the

Planning Board postponed discussion until next week.

vice president, business manager and secretary.

~~each~~. Under the present system, the officers'

is paid by AUS. The payments can be

~~receive~~ tuition ~~scholarships~~.

~~Tuition scholarships are of~~ unequal ~~value,~~

because

Brown said, ~~Out-of-state~~ tuition is $200 more

a for out-of-state residents than for residents of the state.

~~per~~ quarter ~~than in-state tuition~~. For

he said

this reason, the vice president last year,

in effect

~~who was from out of state,~~ was paid more

than the president. ~~who was from in state.~~

~~The amendment would also help stabilize~~

commented that

~~the AUS budget,~~ Brown ~~said.~~ Under the

it is sometimes hard to

present system ~~the variation in salaries~~

prepare a budget before the

~~makes it difficult to budget prior to~~

election of officers.

The amendment would not be effective until the 1969-70 fiscal year, because next year's budget has already been approved, Brown said.

Brown also proposed an amendment that would give Central Board the power, upon the recommendation of the vice president, "to dismiss ~~by a two-thirds vote~~ any commissioner who does not ~~comply with the responsibilities accorded~~ perform the duties assigned him by the vice president and the Constitution." A two-thirds vote would be required.

At present the vice president, ~~who~~ theoretically is in charge of the commissioners, but has no control over them, Brown said. He told the board that it ~~was~~ is difficult to get most commissioners to make their quarterly reports or to ~~follow~~ observe regulations.

~~One board member suggested that the power to recommend impeachment be widened to include all Central Board members, so the power could not be abused by one man.~~

Discussion of ~~both amendments~~ this proposal, too, was ~~tabled~~ postponed until next week. #

Sometimes reorganization is needed for clarity. Here is a paragraph from a story about a student book store:

> Other store employees will receive a five per cent increase in salaries. Larry Hansen, assistant manager, will receive a $1,000 per year increase effective June 1.

Since an assistant manager is an employee, the implication is that Hansen now earns $20,000. That seems a bit high. Had the copyreader raised the logical question, he might have changed the paragraph to read like this:

> Larry Hansen, assistant manager, will receive a $1,000 annual increase effective June 1. Other store employees will get raises of five per cent.

Incidentally, the editor should also have found out what Hansen's salary was before the increase. The amount of the raise doesn't mean much if the base is not mentioned.

Loosely organized details can make the reader work unnecessarily hard. If a story promises a list of items, it should give a list of items. It should not ramble along like this:

> Burlingame said in the school situation there were four factors which affected a child's sense of security. The first was a lack of friendships or his inability to get along with the other children. He said conditions at home often affect a child's school behavior. Besides home relationships, he listed economic conditions, neighborhood situations, and other children as being included in the term. He said the third factor

was a possible personality conflict

between the teacher and child. Academic

problems can also cause a child to

feel insecure.

It's pretty hard to identify the "four factors" on first reading that passage. The copyreader could bring them out this way:

Burlingame said ~~in the school~~

~~situation there were~~ four factors

~~which~~ affect~~ed~~ a child's sense of

at school. He listed them as: (1)

security ~~The first was a~~ lack of

friendships or ~~his~~ inability to get

along with the other children. ~~He~~

(2) Home including personal

~~said~~ conditions ~~at home often affect~~

~~a child's school behavior. Besides~~

~~home~~ relationships, ~~he listed~~ economic

conditions, neighborhood situations,

and other children. ~~as being included~~

~~in the term. He said the third factor~~

(3)

~~was a possible~~ personality conflict

(4)

between the teacher and child. Academic

problems. ~~can also cause a child to~~

~~feel insecure.~~

What seems to be poor organization may be merely the lack of a transitional sentence or phrase. A lot of stories about people begin with descriptive material instead of a name, like this:

A 10-year-old Atlanta boy saved his dog from drowning yesterday and then. . . .

The pilot of a hijacked airliner said today that. . . .

The party was over today for an armored car guard accused of. . . .

Such a descriptive opening is usually followed, in the second paragraph, by a name, like this:

A bearded gunman held up the manager of the Good Samaritan Loan Co. today and fled with $2,548.

Henry Goodluck pursued the man into the street, caught him after a two-block chase, and persuaded him to return the money.

Henry Goodluck is the loan company manager, of course. Or is he? Maybe he's a customer, or a shareholder, or a maintenance man, or a stranger who walked into the building by mistake. The reader can't be sure. In this common situation, the copyreader can help by editing this way:

A bearded gunman held up the manager of the Good Samaritan Loan Co. today and fled with $2,548.

(The manager,)
Henry Goodluck pursued the man into the street, caught him after a two-block chase, and persuaded him to return the money.

The reader now has a bridge to carry him from the first paragraph to the second.

Once in a while a reporter, like any storyteller, wastes a punch line by using it prematurely. Here is a passage from a feature story about 6-year-olds and their reactions to prints of famous paintings:

```
        The teacher turned to Whistler's
"Portrait of My Mother." All the children
agreed that she was twenty two.
        "She's a grandma because her face
is old," said a boy.
        "I think she's George Washington's
wife," said another.
        "She gives people candy because
she's old," said a little girl.
```

This is what an editor did to help it:

```
       [The teacher turned to Whistler's
"Portrait of My Mother." ~~All the children
agreed that she was twenty two.~~
       ["She's a grandma because her face
is old," said a boy.
       ["I think she's George Washington's
wife," said another.
       ["She gives people candy because
she's old," said a little girl.
       [All the children agreed that
she was 22 ⊗
```

Content

```
     Lars Tootle, a junior in the College
of Education, likes his hamburgers well
done.  When asked why, he said, "Because
they taste better."
     Tootle said he realizes some people
like hamburgers medium rare, and still
others prefer them rare.
     "I have no argument with these folks,"
he said.  "As a matter of fact, I used
to take my own hamburgers slightly on
the rare side."
     Tootle said he tried a well-done
hamburger while visiting Hemisfair in San Antonio
in 1968, and liked it.  He's been eating
them that way ever since.
     He added that he usually drinks
root beer when he has a hamburger,
but pointed out that once in a while
he has a cherry Coke.
```

That story never appeared in a college newspaper, but it might have. It typifies the Mickey Mouse feature that shouldn't make it but sometimes does because it's lying around the office and there is a hole to fill. A good copy desk would make sure that such a piece didn't lie around long enough to get set in type, however. While the ultimate decision on whether or not to use a story may not be his, the copyreader has an obligation to call a worthless item to the attention of the responsible editor.

We have already seen that the copyreader can help refine a meaningless generality by asking the reporter for specifics. He should also make sure that the story is complete, that it raises no questions that it doesn't answer, that it has enough detail, that it is consistent within itself, and that it reports the facts on which its interpretive comment, if any, is based. He should also make sure that the story is not cluttered with meaningless detail, does not waste time on the obvious, and is free from irrelevancies.

There is a huge hole in this story:

> Common Pleas Judge Howard Goldsberry handed down a temporary restraining order Friday against the City of Chillocothe until hearings can be had on the petition of Donald J. and Zelma M. Snyder, 569 Johnson Road, on alleged illegal assessments.
>
> Represented by attorney John S. Street Jr., the Snyders claim that assessments against their property for water and sanitary sewer lines are illegal and void because the city did not serve notice upon them of passage of the assessment resolution, and because they were already being served by water and sewer lines, and the new lines are of no benefit.

Despite its inclusion of minutiae such as the name of the plaintiffs' lawyer, the story overlooks two basic facts: what the Snyders' petition asks the court to do, and what the court has restrained the city from doing. A natural oversight for the reporter, perhaps, but one the copyreader should have caught.

And here's a wire story, with a local angle, that fairly shouts a question:

> BOZEMAN (AP) — Donald F. Aldrich, Missoula, was awarded the Governor's Award Thursday as conservationist of the year, Ken Baldwin, awards committee chairman, said.
>
> Baldwin said the award and eight others were made for 1967 by the National Wildlife Federation. Each recipient gets a statuette and a citation.
>
> Robert C. Lynam, Miles City, was given the wildlife award. John M. Schroeder, Lolo, received the soil award.
>
> The water conservation award went to Frank Dunkle of Helena, director of the Montana Fish and Game Department, and the education award to Elmore Smith of Alberton.

Harold Miller of Sanders received the communications award and the Montana Wilderness Association of Bozeman got the organization award.

Maurice Boorman, Kalispell, received the forest award. Rep. John L. Delano, R-Helena, received the legislation award.

The big question for Missoula readers was this: what did Mr. Aldrich do to entitle him to the top award? His hometown paper went to the trouble of carrying his picture with the story but did not follow through on this critical point.

Neither AP nor UPI can possibly carry all the details that are of concern to all members and clients. When there is a local angle, the individual newspaper must often chase after the details. The paper may completely rewrite the story, if it wishes, to provide local emphasis.

It is sometimes easier to spot a little hole in a story. A big hole may be hidden by the context or camouflaged by detail, whereas the little hole is often outlined by the material around it. Even so, it isn't always filled, as this strange passage shows:

Several other unidentified persons,

including a University football player,

were allegedly attacked by the man.

The copyreader might have wondered how an unidentified person could be identified as a football player. The best guess is that the police said the man was a football player but declined to give his name. Whatever the fact is, the newspaper reader should not be made to wonder what member of the squad was involved. If the name wasn't available, the passage could have been edited this way:

Several other ~~unidentified~~ persons,

~~including a University football player,~~

~~were~~ allegedly were attacked by the man.

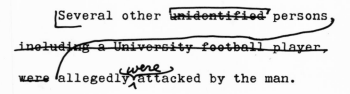

When a passage is sure to raise a question in the reader's mind, the story should answer the question or explain why no answer is available. If it can't do either, the copyreader should delete the troublesome material.

The need for explanation arises in stories that call for comment by a public official, by someone involved in a controversy, or by an expert on a subject in the news. When the need is clear and the comment unobtainable, the story can answer the reader's question by saying "The governor declined to comment," "The mayor could not be reached for comment," "The senator said he would not comment until he had read the statement," or "The dean said it was a private matter and it would be improper for him to comment."

Some stories are incomplete because they are vague or deal in generalities. When the problem is caused by sloppy reporting, the copyreader usually can't do much about it. But when loose writing or oversight is the cause, he can do a lot by asking questions. The answers may be in the reporter's notes or at the other end of a telephone line.

There are types and degrees of vagueness. Sometimes the vocabulary is so fuzzy that it's meaningless. Here are two cases in point:

> An unusually small number of floats appeared this year.
>
> After adequate Biblical training, she joined the Campus Crusade for Christ.

Obviously, a "small number" of floats could be 7 or 18 or 122, and only the reader who has been an annual observer of the event will know what the writer means.

"Adequate Biblical training" could mean different things to different readers, and nothing at all to some. The reporter should say where the girl went to Bible school, and for how long.

The general adjectives—"small," "large," "few," "many," "light," "heavy"—must be used with care because they are relative and subject to interpretation. A hot day at the South Pole is not the same as a hot day in New Orleans, a crowd that seems small to Spiro Agnew might seem large to Hubert Humphrey, and a little girl may be a tall 6-year-old to one man, and a short teen-ager to another.

Some passages are specific enough to mean something, but too general to mean much. Some examples:

> The seasons of the year also influence how much interest a student will have in a course.
>
> When the men are selected, they go through a difficult six-week training course which prepares them for all types of rescue and firefighting work.

> The University rifle range does not meet National Rifle Association standards.
>
> Mexican students are more strictly regulated than American students in such things as dress and hours.
>
> Questions directed to him were of the usual political nature.
>
> The stained-glass windows in churches today are not as good as the ones made in the last century, Dr. Klassen continued.

There is nothing wrong with those sentences, as far as they go. But, lacking additional information, the reader must wonder:

Which are the good seasons for student interest and which are the bad and why the difference?

What do the men *do* in the six-week training course? What's so hard about it?

What's the matter with the rifle range? Too short? Too narrow? Muddy pits? Unsafe?

How are dress and hours regulated in Mexico? Does the University prescribe what can be worn at given times? Does it order everyone to his room at 7 p.m.?

What is a question of "the usual" political nature?

In what ways are modern stained-glass windows not as good as those of the nineteenth century?

There's a good chance that the reporter has the answers to questions like those. The copyreader should ask.

Professional jargon can blur the picture, and the reporter who has talked to the jargonist may be so bemused that he doesn't realize how strange the language is when he repeats it. Some examples:

> The camp tries to be community-centered so the boys can find jobs and live independently when they are released.
>
> The medical personnel can relieve tension caused by the disease process, but the financial implications remain.
>
> The goal of the rehabilitation center is to restore the patient's highest level of function.

The problems illustrated here are the results of specialized vocabulary and professional pomposity. The terms "community-centered" and "highest level of function" may have instant meaning to the sociologist and the rehabilitation worker, but they will cause most other readers to pause. The passage about tension relief and financial implications probably means something like this:

> Doctors and nurses can give the patient hope of recovery, but he still must face the financial problems caused by a long stay in the hospital.

The writer can also blur the picture by reporting his conclusions while neglecting the facts on which those conclusions are based. "He seemed to have indigestion, acted amused, and apparently suffered a dizzy spell" is less vivid than "He hiccupped, laughed, and toppled to the ground." Here are some roundabout generalities that should be fixed:

> He carried himself with an air of importance.

(Did he strut? Swagger? Prance?)

> The room was sloppy.

(Paper on the floor? Ashtrays full?)

> The many students and faculty present made an appreciative audience.

(Did they roar with laughter? Clap until their hands were blue? Bear the speaker off on their shoulders?)

Stories on speeches are sometimes unnecessarily vague because the reporter describes the speaker's remarks instead of reporting what they were, like this:

> Explaining the history and nature of the Russian-Chinese conflict, Mr. Salisbury pointed out the advantages of a split between these two massive Communist powers. At the same time he showed how the problem was leading to armed conflict which would probably involve nuclear warfare.

This is sort of like writing that "Homer Breakaway, shifty halfback, showed how useful he is to the team and how tough it is for the opposition to win when he is playing well." What the reader wants to know is what Breakaway did to deserve this accolade, and how the game came out. Similarly, in the example above he wants to know what advantages the correspondent pointed out and the reasons for his belief that the problem is leading to armed conflict. The passage could go like this:

> Salisbury said the Sino-Russian split may benefit the United States by blocking a massive anti-American alliance, but he warned that China's fear of a joint Soviet-American attack might lead her to start a nuclear war.

Here are other examples of unnecessary vagueness in speech reporting:

> He spoke at length on the subject of the War on Poverty, its reasons for existence, and the duties of the student as a citizen of the world.

(But what did he *say*?)

> He argued that the battle for peace
>
> needs to be started in the United States,
>
> where a good example should be set.

(Example of *what*? If he was talking about race relations, the story should say so.)

The paragraph on the War on Poverty says nothing, and chances are the copyreader could kill it without harm to the story. He could probably salvage the peace paragraph this way:

> He argued that the battle for peace
>
> should ~~needs to~~ be started in the United States,
>
> with a solution of the race crisis
>
> ~~where a good example should be set.~~

Vagueness results from a reporter's failure to give instances of glorious, or dull, generalities. When it's a matter of oversight rather than inept reporting, the copyreader can help by asking the reporter for examples.

A feature story about a student who had spent several months attending school in Switzerland reported:

```
        Social activities are centered within
    the student's family and not among his friends.
```

American students might well be interested in the social activities of the Swiss student. The story needs a couple of examples of social life in the home, and perhaps some examples of American social activities that are foreign to Switzerland.

A story about a student who had dropped out of a military academy said:

```
        The biggest problem was that the cadets
    did not have enough say in matters.
```

An interesting point, but only if it is followed up by examples of the "matters" in which the cadets did not have enough say.

A story about a training program for American Indians said:

```
        Dr. Pope admitted that the program
    had had its dropouts, but expressed confi-
    dence that this situation could be improved
    by better screening and orientation of ap-
    plicants out on the reservations.
```

That's passable, perhaps, but it's not as clear as it would be if it were buttressed by specific examples of Indians who had dropped out, and by comment about what was wrong with the screening.

Nothing frustrates a reader more than an unanswered question. When a power failure left a dozen students trapped in an elevator between floors in a dormitory, a student newspaper reported that "Dean Milton Overholt rescued most of them." Period. A city newspaper, reporting on the work of volunteers at a forest fire, said that "unlike most of the firefighters, McCullough had on slacks and a white shirt." Period.

Some reporting is deliberately incomplete. A paper reports a death in "a local hospital," a brawl in "a South High Street bar," an accident involving "a late-model sedan," or a film that is playing in "a downtown theater." Such vagueness is a matter of policy, and unfortunately the policy of vagueness is widespread. It is rooted in a misguided desire to protect a person or an institution or a business, or to prevent giving "free publicity" to a person, product, or enterprise.

Whatever the reason, it is hard to justify a violation of the principle that a newspaper should publish the news. If the editor feels that the place of death or the scene of a brawl or the make of a car or the availability of a film is not news, that is his judgment. But he should be consistent and see that the entire reference is deleted. If it is not, logic demands that all references be named. There is no reason to "protect" a hospital or a tavern or a hotel when it is in the news. It is absurd to think that its involvement in a crash is good publicity for a car of a particular make. And if mentioning a theater is a free plug, well, that's show biz. Deleting the name is as illogical as using an airbrush to blot out a store sign that appears in a news picture of a downtown parade on Veterans Day. Editors have been known to do that, too.

No matter what the paper's policy is, the copyreader should make sure that the handling is consistent. If one car in a two-car smashup is identified by make, the other should be, too. If one driver's age is given the other's should be, too. Sometimes, when it is impossible to get complete details, there are compelling reasons for carrying limited information. If the age of one driver were unavailable, it would still be appropriate to note that the other was 103.

Just as he looks for the specific to back up the general, the copyreader looks for the *why* to back up the *what*. The *why* is often more interesting. A passage like this one doesn't mean much:

> Present members hope some day the Repertory Theater will be divorced from the University and will be independent, Dr. Brown said.

The unanswered questions are: Why? What's the matter with being associated with the University? If the reporter doesn't have the answers in his notes, there's always the telephone.

Identification by race involves a number of questions of policy and ethics. Until a few years ago it was the general rule on most newspapers outside the South to describe a person as white or black or red or yellow only when race or color was relevant to the story. That is still a widely observed rule, but it has become harder to apply because opinions on the relevance of race differ so widely.

One thing is clear: to some whites and some blacks, skin color is always relevant. To most Americans, skin color is relevant more often than it was a decade ago. The reporter and the editor must let their consciences guide them.

Finally, in checking a story for completeness, the copyreader should make sure that the reporter has left no ends open. If a person or an organization has proposed some sort of action, the story should let the reader know where the matter rests. If a decision has been deferred, the story should say so. Here are a couple of examples, from student newspapers, of stories that just trail off:

> The Associated Women Students' Senate yesterday discussed the possibility of a $1.50 increase in the activity fee of women students as a possible solution to future problems.

(Questions: What can the Associated Women Students do to get a fee increase? Did the discussion fade into coffee and cookies, or did the AWS decide to resume it later, or refer the matter to committee, or what?)

```
        A dance at the College Inn was sug-
    gested at Program Council yesterday to re-
    place the usual "Friday at 4" in the Grill
    next week.  Andrea Grauman, Program Council
    director, said there would be an admission
    charge of 25 cents for the dance from 4 to
    5 p.m., and that she was looking into having
    a Seattle band, "The Jack, King and Queen,"
    play for it.
```

(Questions: Is there going to be a dance or isn't there? If the matter is still up in the air, who will make the decision? When? On what basis?)

While the copyreader should make sure that the package is neatly tied, he should cut off excess string. Many people resist the suggestion that, when they have written everything they have to write, they should stop writing. Yet there is seldom any point in summarizing or repeating. A 400-word story about a United States senator's demand for a new American policy toward China wound up with this:

```
        There is need for a new look at this
    firmly established world power, he said.
```

Since the entire speech dealt with that idea, it is foolish repetition.

The kind of information needed about age, home town, street address, occupation, year in school or college, major field of study, and the like differs from story to story. In most cases, something more than name is needed for full identification, and the copyreader should be alert to spotting the person who is important to a story but comes through as little more than a shadow because of too few identifying details.

If a story calls someone young but doesn't give his age, the copyreader should check on it. "Young" by itself doesn't mean much. Nor does "longtime resident" or "employee of Quire & Ream" when "resident for 76 years" or "office manager of Quire & Ream, stationery suppliers" could be reported just as easily. One would not normally refer to the late Sen. Everett Dirksen as "a longtime employee of the federal government." The same principle applies to persons of lesser stature.

All general descriptions of age—"young," "youthful," "middle aged," "elderly," "aged"—should be handled with care because the reader interprets them subjectively. A 56-year-old man may be "elderly" to a child, but he's only "middle aged" to his 45-year-old friend. The term "youth" generally applies to males between 14 and 20. A "young woman" may be anyone up to about 39, depending upon the context, but it's startling to read about a "young mother" and then find that she is 35. A 43-year-old person is not generally thought of as a "young man," yet John F. Kennedy at that age was referred to, quite properly, as "the young President."

The copyreader should also be skeptical of stories that describe women as "pretty," "attractive," or "beautiful" unless there is photographic evidence. That is not to say that such adjectives are useless. Only that caution is advisable, particularly when the lady under discussion is a gangster's girl friend, a roustabout, a bank president, or a district attorney.

Anonymity should be kept to a minimum. If a plaintiff's lawyer is worth a reference in the story, he's worth a reference by name. This point may seem obvious, but it's easy to read over the omission of a name in constructions like "Amick's coach said that . . ." or "LaGrande's son denied that his father . . ." or "The jury foreman reported that. . . ."

Sometimes anonymity is deliberate or unavoidable. But the "spokesman" or "source" or "person close to the program who asked not to be identified" is never as credible as a person who is named. And it takes a lot of skill for a writer to breathe life into an anonymous main character in a story, whether it's a pot smoker or a confessed cheater or an unwed mother or a stool pigeon.

In a story in a college newspaper, a foreign student criticized the "cowardice" of other foreign students who, he said, were afraid to criticize the United States. He then made a forthright adverse criticism of the United States, but declined to be identified. His words had little impact.

In another story, a self-described dope addict wouldn't allow his name to be used. That was understandable, but his story, based on a fictitious name, seemed unreal.

The copyreader can't ask a reporter to violate a confidence, but he can raise a question. Sometimes the anonymity is inadvertent.

Detail is important to a story, but so is pace—its rate of movement or degree of energy. The passive voice can kill pace, as can wordiness and too much detail. Hence the copyreader should be on the lookout for minor details that deaden rather than enliven. The story that says that dinner got under way "at 7 p.m. sharp" or that "the minutes were approved as read" isn't going to hold readers long. Nor is the story that drones through chronological minutiae, like this one:

```
     Mrs. Linda Coleman, Homecoming Queen
of 1966, came forward and said a few words
of thanks for her election last year.  She was
joined by Loren Haarr, student body presi-
dent.  Pat Holmes, chairman of Homecoming,
then brought the envelope containing the
Homecoming Queen's name.  Loren Haarr read off
Sheila MacDonald's name.
```

If the copyreader felt that the story had to include the names of Mrs. Coleman, Mr. Haarr, and Miss Holmes, he could have made it read like this:

> After brief remarks by Linda Coleman, last year's Homecoming queen, Student Body President Loren Haarr read the new queen's name from a paper handed to him by Pat Holmes, Homecoming chairman.

Biographical detail is appropriate to an advance story about a speech, but it does little for a story about the speech itself. An advance on a talk by Malcolm Muggeridge might include paragraphs about his education, publications, and editorial jobs, but the report of his talk might well identify him only as a British journalist or satirist or former editor of *Punch.*

Nor does it add much to report that Mr. Muggeridge's topic was "The World We Live In—A Fool's Eye View." The title might be informative in a story announcing that the speaker would speak, but after his talk it's a little like writing: "In a talk entitled 'Why We Should Raise Taxes,' Gov. Buffoon yesterday urged the legislature to impose a 90 percent tax on individual incomes."

The reporter who unnecessarily puts himself in a story just clutters things. The personal experience story can have impact, though, and when the reporter is part of the story he should write himself into it. (In the first person, too. Not as "this reporter" or "we" or "an observer.") But when his role is merely that of chronicler, he should stay out.

Here's how one college reporter began a feature story:

> The first time I saw Dr. Richard D. Burk, he was in a lecture class at Dodd Hall, where he holds the position of director of rehabilitation for the Ohio State University. His quick humor, warm smile and sparkling blue eyes immediately drew my attention from the crutches which supported him to the man himself. My attention soon grew into a desire to find out more about this man who, rendered a paraplegic by polio, had overcome his handicap and attained a full and useful life.

The trouble here is that the writer is standing between Dr. Burk and the reader. While the story is ostensibly about Dr. Burk, what the reader is getting is a story about the reporter's desire to learn about him. The copyreader might suggest that the reporter get out of the way and rewrite the opening like this:

> Dr. Richard D. Burk's quick humor, warm smile and sparkling blue eyes make people forget that he uses crutches. Polio made him a paraplegic. Today, 15 years after being stricken, he is director of rehabilitation at the Ohio State University.

Another way to say too much in a story is to point out the obvious. Some writers just don't know when to stop, particularly if they are writing about a specialized field. An example is this paragraph taken from a pamphlet distributed by a dental society to the parents of school children:

> With the eruption of all four wisdom teeth, the individual will have a complete set of 32 permanent teeth. In some cases, one or more six-year molars may be lost early in life, or due to an accident, a front tooth may be lost. This person will not have 32 teeth even if all wisdom teeth erupt.

The obvious is usually injected more subtly than that. When a ship was denied entry to the United States, its captain threatened to dump his cargo of giraffes and other wild animals into the sea. During the controversy that followed, one newspaper reported:

> The cud-chewing animals, unaware of the congressional uproar over their fate, are due to arrive on Tuesday.

One wonders what might have happened aboard ship had someone warned the animals of their danger.

At the opposite extreme is the unwarranted conclusion. The copyreader should guard against interpretation that goes beyond the facts. A newspaper reported:

> Columbus area doctors, for the most part, are angered by an edict by the Ohio Department of Public Welfare that they swear to uphold the Civil Rights Act or be denied payment for treating welfare patients.

This broad statement was substantiated by the comments of three doctors, all of them anonymous. The Columbus telephone directory has listings for more than nine hundred physicians and osteopaths. The copyreader should have spotted this weakness. If the three were representative of a larger group, the story should have reported how many of the area's physicians were polled, and by whom.

The "opinion survey" story often has this flaw. If the reporter has made only a spot check, his results may be interesting and worth reporting but they still lack validity as a poll of opinion. The copyreader should not let twenty randomly selected coeds go through as "most coeds."

Euphemisms are designed to avoid giving offense to readers. This is a laudable motive, and although some argue that a death is a death and not a "passage" it must be conceded that, if an editor feels a change in language is essential to good taste, his argument is as good as the next man's.

Taste is a matter of opinion, and it's impossible to lay down rules about it. Some editors feel that any form of profanity is out of place in a general circulation newspaper. Others permit almost anything. In between, and probably most numerous, are the editors who feel that mild profanity is all right so long as it adds needed meaning or appropriate flavor to a story.

Whatever the policy is, it should be a forthright one and not the cowardly compromise that is represented by dashes: "Mr. Peppercorn said he'd be d----d if he would let anyone call him a --- -- - ----- without telling him to go to h---." While the decision on this kind of foolishness is usually made at a higher editorial level, the copyreader can at least suggest that the passage be edited to read, "Peppercorn said he wouldn't let anyone call him names without replying in kind."

Differences in taste are reflected in newspaper policies on pictures of gruesome accidents and pretty girls, in the use of detail in stories of violence, in the coverage of domestic quarrels, in decisions on the dividing line between the public interest and invasion of privacy, and in countless other questions that each paper must decide on in accordance with its conscience. The copyreader's role here is pretty much that of watchdog. He should make enough noise, when bad taste seems to be prowling about, to alert the responsible editor. Certainly he should raise a question when a writer's attempt at brightness turns into ridicule of misfortune, as it did here:

> Three nurses at Sacred Heart Hospital got a taste of their own medicine yesterday when they were seriously injured in a one-car accident on Hamilton Street.

Or when some shocking detail in a story appears to get undue emphasis, as in this wire service lead about the hijacking of an airliner:

> PARIS (AP) — A passenger on a hijacked Israeli airliner that was forced down in Algiers Tuesday by Arab commandoes said one of the hijackers tasted a drop of blood of an injured crewman and said, "It's good, the blood of Israelis."

Both passages call for editorial judgment. The point is that, if the copyreader senses that something is wrong, his opinion should be part of the editorial decision, if only to the extent that he brings the problem to someone's attention.

Backgrounding

THE writer and editor should assume that the reader has just returned from a long canoe trip and needs background on every running story. If a murder trial is in progress, he will want to read about the latest developments, but he will also need the basic background facts: the identities of the defendant and the victim, the date and place of the crime, the circumstances surrounding the killing, what has happened in the trial so far, the name of the judge and the principal lawyers, and the makeup of the jury by sex and race, if these facts are relevant.

The reader who has been following the case from day to day probably does not need or want all that. Nevertheless, for every issue there are some readers who have read nothing previously about the event, others who have not read much, and others who would like to have their memories refreshed.

To illustrate the benefits of backgrounding, let's look at two hypothetical reports of a hypothetical trial.

> Penelope Wilson, a waitress at the Blue Moon Cafe, testified in District Court today that she saw Philip J. Hess in the cafe on the night of May 5.
>
> Mrs. Wilson, a prosecution witness, said she believed Hess entered at about 5:30 p.m. and remained until about 9:45.
>
> She testified that she served him between 15 and 20 cups of coffee while he sat in a booth.

While this story covers the waitress' testimony thoroughly, it is not very informative. It does not say who is on trial for what offense, and it does not indicate why the testimony is significant. Here is a second version:

> Penelope Wilson, a waitress at the Blue Moon Cafe, testified in District Court today that she served 15 to 20 cups of coffee to Philip J. Hess on the night of May 5.
>
> Mrs. Wilson was the fifth prosecution witness at Hess' trial for murder in the May 5 shooting of Howard Bacon, 75, manager and cook at the Blue Moon.
>
> Hess, a 32-year-old Milltown dentist, is accused of firing five rifle shots into Bacon after the cook refused to draw another cup of coffee for him.
>
> Mrs. Wilson told the court she believes Hess entered the Blue Moon at about 5:30 p.m. and remained there until 9:45. According to previous witnesses, Bacon was shot at about 9:45.

The need for this kind of fill-in may seem obvious, but the failure to provide background is nevertheless a common fault. The reporter's problem is mostly psychological. He can become so familiar with a story that he inadvertently neglects to mention facts that he knows well, or deliberately omits details that he believes are so widely known as to require no repetition.

A school principal may have interesting things to say about the new requirements of a state college of education, but his comments won't mean much to the reader who doesn't know how the new requirements compare to the old.

A survey of public reaction to a police department's attempted censorship of books does not mean much without a review of the action the police have taken.

If a story says that a lawyer has been hired to defend "the students and faculty members arrested in Friday's demonstration," it should explain where the demonstration was, what it was all about, and why arrests were made.

If the mayor has appointed a Human Relations Commission to investigate "the recent incidents," the story should note the nature of the incidents.

If a magistrate is disqualified from hearing a case because he has "been involved as both prosecutor and judge," the story should explain how he got himself involved in the prosecution.

If a coach is interviewed and asked why he had a miserable season, the story should mention the team's record.

If the new president of the Student Senate comments on the closeness of the election, the story should give figures on the vote.

And so forth and so on. There are exceptions, of course. If one issue of a newspaper carries two or more stories on the same event, it's not necessary that each story report the same basic information. A secondary or "sidebar" story may make only passing reference to the main event. In the case of a disaster, for example, a sidebar interview with a survivor or an eyewitness or a rescue worker might simply refer to "yesterday's passenger train derailment at Inferno Gulch," leaving the details about deaths and injuries to the lead story. But when a story stands alone, it should be complete.

Here's one, from a college newspaper, that would make little sense to a reader not familiar with the organizations and issues:

> The CRA agreed last night to meet with SAM to discuss the war in Vietnam.
>
> The CRA said, however, that it would not debate with SAM representatives on the basis of SAM's eight points.
>
> "To debate on their terms would be like debating capital punishment with your hangman," said CRA member Harry DelForte.

A more adequate story would identify the organizations in full, note what they stand for, explain "SAM's eight points," and show the relevance of DelForte's comment, perhaps by lengthening the quotation. It might go like this:

> The Committee for Reasonable Action agreed last night to discuss the war in Vietnam with the Support America group (SAM), but rejected SAM's challenge to "debate" war issues.
>
> SAM, a new organization that supports American intervention in Vietnam, last week challenged the antiwar CRA to debate eight specific questions related to U.S. involvement.
>
> Several CRA members objected to the proposal last night on grounds that SAM's position is fixed.
>
> "To debate on their terms would be like debating capital punishment with your hangman," said CRA member Harry DelForte. "You'd be trapped."

To correct weaknesses in backgrounding may require extensive reorganization, rewriting, and research, for which there often isn't time. But if he can do it, the copyreader should return an incomplete story to the reporter, or insert whatever background material he is able to put together himself.

The job may be easier than it looks at first. For example, a wire service reported the death of a man who had been involved in long-past political scandals. Since no one on the copy desk recalled the man or his scandalous activities, the copyreader figured the story wouldn't mean much to many readers. The solution? The newspaper's library. It produced clippings that permitted the copyreader to write a background paragraph. Thus an empty obituary took on meaning. The whole thing delayed the story about five minutes.

The moral here is that the copyreader shouldn't pass an inadequate story without estimating how much time and effort may be needed to correct it.

Quotations

DIRECT quotations cause trouble. Correctly handled, they brighten a story, increase its credibility, and make it more attractive typographically. Mistreated, as they often are, they deaden a story and make it less believable.

There is no handy rule to help the copyreader decide when to quote directly and when to paraphrase. There are a couple of guidelines, though, that can help him make a judgment:

Use direct quotations to record colorful language, emphasize important or interesting points, ensure accuracy in controversial matters, break up blocks of exposition, and achieve dramatic effect.

Do not use direct quotations to report routine matters of fact or the commonplace things people say, to give information that could be presented more concisely and forcefully by paraphrasing, or to justify the use of unclear statements.

If a person is newsworthy, it doesn't necessarily follow that everything he says is worth reporting. A story about him should be selective. It should develop ideas of importance and interest, but it should ignore the dull, no-account, and stale.

Good copyreading tightens copy by deleting meaningless, drab, and obvious quotations like this one from a janitor who figured in a story about an indoor sports arena:

```
     "I try to help make the arena neat for the
people.  There are eight rest rooms in here.  I
have to get them looking nice before the games."
```

Since most of us would normally expect this type of service from a janitor, the quotation deadens the story instead of brightening it.

Here's another "ho-hum" quote, from an elementary school drama teacher:

> "Last Monday evening we staged 'Cinderella' in French," she said. "We were a smash! We even had a 'Ball Scene.' The hardest part of staging the play was explaining to the 10-year-old boys why they had to learn to waltz."

It would have been enough to note that the teacher's class staged "Cinderella" in French.

These so-what quotes are of a type familiar to all readers of high school and college journals:

> (From a story about a naval ROTC detachment's visit to Washington, D.C.) "I wish all the guys could have gone," Runkleman said.

> (Quoting the husband of the head resident of a women's dormitory) "I take life lightly and like to joke around a lot, and especially like the association with girls."

When a quotation is relevant but seems windy, the editor should decide whether paraphrase or indirect quotation could make the point more effectively.

Here's one from a story on the problems of being a twin in college:

> "Being twins is hardly ever boring," Rob
>
> said. "On one occasion, Ron and I switched dates,
>
> and the girls we were with didn't realize it until
>
> an hour afterwards. It was a real blast!"

The writer could have made the point better this way:

> ~~"Being twins is hardly ever boring,"~~ Rob
>
> said ~~"On one occasion, Ron and I~~ he and Ron once switched dates,
>
> and the girls ~~we were with~~ didn't realize it ~~until~~ for
>
> an hour. ~~afterwards. It was a real blast!"~~

Here's a campus security officer's comment that should be paraphrased because of the torrent of words.

> "Percentagewise, no one group violates the rules more than another," said Mr. Curry. "Naturally, because the students comprise the largest group, we expect to have more student violators, but they're not out of proportion to their number."

This would be better:

> Mr. Curry said that students get the most tickets but that the ratio of tickets to car owners is about the same for all groups.

Direct quotations shouldn't be thrown away on commonplace statements of fact. Examples:

> "I will leave Monday and won't be back until the following Monday," she said.

(Better: She will leave Monday and be gone a week.)

> Sue stated, "In getting information I combine note taking and memorization."

(Better: In writing her story, Sue relies on both notes and memory.)

Don't waste space with quotations that add nothing. An example, from a guidance center psychologist:

> "When a student comes in for help, the first thing I try to do is find out where the problem lies."

(So what else is new?)

If a person has said something that is clearly untrue, the comment should not be passed along as though the paper believed it. And if it's a misstatement or a misquotation, it shouldn't be passed along at all. One story quoted an official as saying that a civil rights leader had spoken "from every church pulpit in Washington, D.C." He couldn't have meant it.

The direct quotation must be believable, and when the reporter has lost the flavor of the news source's speech the copyreader should ask for a rewrite, or change the passage to an indirect quotation. That does not mean that the direct quotation must always be a verbatim account of a person's words. But allowing for condensation, grammatical changes, and minor reorganization, the language should be substantially the speaker's. Here are some supposedly informal quotations that should not have passed the copy desk:

(A policeman speaking)

> "We are happiest when we are fully used in the service of some worthwhile enterprise."

(An airline passenger recalling a bad moment aloft)

> "In tense expectation the crew and passengers continued in silence throughout the night. Much excitement and relief was felt by all when we saw the sunrise over the mainland of New England."

(An athlete, reporting on locker room lore)

> "I can't believe the speed at which that trainer can work, unrolling tapes and taping ankles while all the time talking to the guys about their individual problems."

(A student of veterinary medicine)

> "Contrary to much public opinion, the recipient of a doctor of veterinary medicine degree, after a rigorous four-year program in which he learns the animal sciences and various public health principles, may enter successfully into a number of different fields."

(A convalescent)

> "At the time of the accident I felt both embarrassment and apprehension."

Unless there's a reason for reporting nonsense (to let a politician hang himself with his own words, for example, or to report the intentional absurdities of a comedian), the desk shouldn't pass quotations, however accurate, that are incomprehensible. Here's one, from an interview with a dean of women, that makes the mind boggle:

> She arrived in Prague the day the president resigned. "A flag that flies constantly over the capital was missing, but that was the only outward appearance that the country was without a leader," she said.

A comma-chaser might pass the passage, but a thoughtful copyreader would note the implication that one of the Czech president's chores is to hoist the flag. The editor should get the reporter to clarify the lady's statement, or delete the quotation.

The desk shouldn't pass the nonsensical indirect quotation, either. Another travel story provides an example:

> Miss Clow noted that Russia's moral education of their young people is much more noticeable in that country than here, but she qualified that statement by adding, "What is moral education?"

The implication is that the lady is judging matters she can't define. That alone is enough to make the quotation unprintable. Beyond that, one wonders why the education of Russians *shouldn't* be more noticeable in Russia than in the United States.

Closely allied to the nonsense quote is the one so full of jargon, wind, bad grammar, or incomprehensible phrasing that the point doesn't come through.

When the copyreader comes upon an incomprehensible direct quotation, he should ask the reporter to write a comprehensible paraphrase, write one himself, or delete the passage. In the case of an incomprehensible paraphrase, he should have the reporter rewrite the passage, or delete it.

At times the copyreader must go back to the reporter because the quotation is incomplete. The reporter may be unable to add enough to save the quote, but the desk should always try.

A couple of examples, one quoting a race driver and the other a wilderness researcher, illustrate the problem:

> He said, "I'm never satisfied after a race. I feel I've never reached the ultimate in racing."

(Why isn't he satisfied? What's an example of something he wishes he'd done differently? What does he mean by "the ultimate in racing"? Without these details, the basic quotation means little.)

> Don said: "Frank and I took every precaution for our safety. While living on the mountain we did various exercise experiments and made periodic tests."

(This would mean something if Don named a couple of precautions and described a few exercises and tests. As it stands, however, the passage is worthless.)

In addition to making sure that quoted material is worthwhile, makes sense, and is believable, the copyreader should see that it fits into the story logically, and should watch for mechanical flaws.

One case in point:

```
     Student body president Loren Haarr said of
the proposed pamphlet on student rights:  "Central
boards and student governments are suffering
across the country because they spend time on
limited objectives.  The whole state can benefit
from this research dealing with student and
administrative problems in terms of legality."
```

The copyreader who takes this statement apart will see that it says this:

```
     Student body president Loren Haarr said the
pamphlet will be useful to students at all schools
and colleges in the state.
```

Another example, taken from a report of a student political meeting:

```
     He commented on Mansfield's stand on the
voting age, saying Mansfield advocated the lower
voting age when he spoke at the University because
he had taken opportunity of an area where he
thought it would do him some good.
```

The speaker was apparently accusing the senator of expediency. The copyreader might make the passage read:

```
     He charged that Mansfield, in endorsing a
lower voting age, sought only to curry favor
among college students.
```

Sometimes a quotation seems to be out of context because the reporter has not related it to the speaker's basic points.

A student newspaper quoted Hubert Humphrey, then vice president, as saying nice things about two congressmen. Since the two were not identified as candidates for reelection, the reader might have wondered why the vice president had singled them out. The same story quoted Humphrey as saying: "No administration expects a senator to stand right behind every administration policy, all the time." The quotation was accurate but meant little because the story did not note that Humphrey was defending a senator who was at loggerheads with the president.

A direct quotation often makes more sense if it follows and supports a paraphrase than if it stands alone, without introduction. The Humphrey quote just cited, for example, would have been more understandable if it had been handled like this:

> Humphrey defended Sen. Metcalf's right to oppose the administration's policies in Vietnam. "No administration expects a senator to stand right behind every administration policy, all the time," he said.

The opposite of the isolated, out-of-context quotation is the overquote. It often represents tactical surrender by the reporter. He has turned his story over to his source and relieved himself of the responsibility and risk of telling the story himself. The news source has thus become, in effect, the reporter. The danger is not so much that the news report will be slanted as that it will be wordy and unclear.

An excerpt from a story on a speech by a political candidate illustrates the problem:

> "There is no one to answer for unsafe highway design in the state," he said. "The accident at Bowman's Corners last year was the result of faulty highway design and lack of warning. Nothing was done to remedy the situation until after the accident. A few people are making all the decisions. The theory of free enterprise is that power is delegated to make decisions, but with this authority goes the responsibility to answer for what you do or don't do. We have lost this in the state.
>
> "The trouble with state government is two-fold. People don't know what's going on in the state government, and secondly state government is now not responsible to the electorate for its

actions. If I were elected I would coordinate state boards and commissions in such a manner that these groups would be responsible to the people of the state.

"In the past, the state boards were not responsible to anyone for their actions. For example, take the Railroad and Public Service Commission, which is responsible for establishing rates for public utilities. Members are elected in staggered six-year terms every two years. A member elected to the commission votes for the public utility for the first four years he's in office, and then votes for the public's interests the next two years to guarantee reelection."

The person who wrote that was a tape recorder masquerading as a reporter. Any stenographer could have done as well. Admittedly, to fix this passage on the desk in the face of a deadline is a real problem.

But here is one approach:

Anderson charged that the accident which killed five persons at Bowman's Corners last year was caused by faulty highway design and lack of warning. He said the situation was symptomatic of a basic ailment of state government: lack of responsibility.

"A few people are making all the decisions," he said. "The theory of free enterprise is that power to make decisions is delegated, but with this authority goes the responsibility to answer for what you do or don't do."

Anderson argued that the state has "lost" responsible government because the system of state boards and commissions prevents the people from knowing what is going on, and protects state officials from being responsible to the people for their actions.

He cited the Railroad and Public Service Commission as being particularly insulated from the public. A member elected for a six-year term, he said, typically votes for the utilities' interests his first four years and then swings to the public side for two years to assure his reelection. Since the three members are elected on a staggered basis, one being named every two years, the utilities are assured of a majority at all times, Anderson said.

"If I were elected," he declared, "I would coordinate state boards and commissions so that they would be responsible to the people of the state."

It may be objected, with justification, that this is rewriting, not editing. However, editing alone can produce a passage that is substantially the same as the rewrite. Like this:

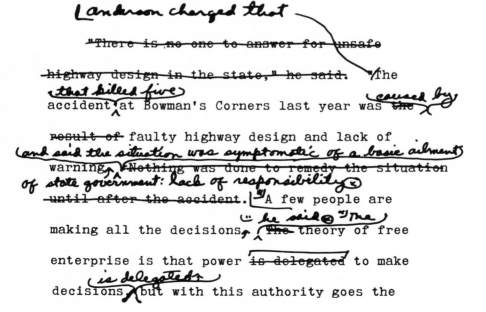

Anderson charged that

~~"There is no one to answer for unsafe~~

~~highway design in the state," he said.~~ "The

that killed five

accident at Bowman's Corners last year was ~~the~~ caused by

~~result of~~ faulty highway design and lack of

and said the situation was symptomatic of a basic ailment

warning, ~~"Nothing was done to remedy the situation~~

of state government: lack of responsibility.

~~until after the accident.~~ "A few people are

he said. "The

making all the decisions, ~~The~~ theory of free

enterprise is that power ~~is delegated~~ to make

is delegated

decisions, but with this authority goes the

responsibility to answer for what you do or don't

do." ~~We have lost this in the state.~~

Anderson argued that the state has "lost" responsible government because the system of state boards and commissions prevents the people from knowing what is going on and protects state officials from bein

~~"The trouble with state government is two-~~

~~fold. People don't know what's going on in the~~

~~state government, and secondly state government~~

~~is now not responsible to the electorate for its~~

~~actions. If I were elected I would coordinate~~

~~state boards and commissions in such a manner~~

~~that these groups would be~~ responsible to the

people ~~of the state.~~ for their actions.

He cited ~~"In the past,~~ ~~the state boards were not~~

~~responsible to anyone for their actions. For~~

~~example, take~~ the Railroad and Public Service

Commission, which is responsible for establishing

rates for public utilities, as being particularly insulated from the public. ~~M~~Members ~~are~~ elected

in staggered six-year terms every two years, he said. A

member ~~elected to the commission~~ typically votes for the

~~public~~ utility interests for the first four years ~~he's~~ he is in

office, and then votes for the public's interests

the next two years to guarantee reelection."

Fragmentary quotations are the source of a common writing error: the use of the third person when grammar and logic demand the first. The writer probably doesn't realize that he is shifting his point of view in mid-sentence. Whatever the reason, the copyreader should be ready to fix this kind of passage:

> Neville Tucker resigned from the Board of Education last night, calling sentiments expressed by Negro parents of Shawnee Elementary School pupils in a public meeting "a repudiation of all he has stood for."

If we are to believe this, we must believe that Mr. Tucker referred to himself as "he." Since that seems most unlikely, the copyreader should step in. He has three options:

(1) Change the "he has" to "I have"
(2) Put quotation marks around only the words "a repudiation"
(3) Remove the quotation marks entirely.

The language of a passage may restrict the choices. A sports writer once wrote of a defeated boxer:

> He said that even after he was back on his feet, he "felt like he was in a transom or something."

Obviously, it would not help matters here to strike out the quotation marks.

Fragmentary direct and indirect quotations can lead to jarring repetition, particularly when they are in the lead. Here's an example:

> ROCHESTER, N.Y. (AP) — Virginia Aitken, who went to Formosa three years ago to become a Buddhist nun, is back home and said Friday she has returned to Christianity.
>
> "I have returned to Christianity," Miss Aitken, 23, said.

Most "quotation stammer" is harder to spot than that. It is often buried deeper in the story, and as the copyreader moves from the lead his absorption with other problems may let him read right over it. It'll hit the reader, though.

The copyreader should never pass a quotation without consciously checking the punctuation. Reporters usually type the opening quotation mark, but they often forget to close the quote, and they may not remember the convention that quotation marks always go outside the period and the comma.

The language used by the person being quoted sometimes creates a problem. If a coach predicts, "We'll blast hell out of 'em," good taste and the policy of the paper will be the copyreader's guide in deciding whether to quote him fully or to change the quotation to "We'll blast them."

But if the coach says, after a come-from-behind victory, "Our team don't never quit," the editor has a stickier problem. The quote may not offend anyone and is probably relevant to the postgame story. The question is, though, does the paper use the bad grammar or does it make the quotation read "Our team never quits" or does it paraphrase, reporting that the coach praised his boys for not quitting?

Most newsmen would probably clean up the grammar and leave in the quotation marks. Even though not completely accurate, the quotation would convey the coach's meaning and the exuberant spirit of the remark.

If the coach had a reputation for colorful mutilation of the language, most newsmen would probably let the bad grammar stand. In general, copy desks clean up the language when the miscues are inadvertent or offensive, but let them stand when they are relevant to the facts or to the tone of the story.

A word of caution: the copyreader may be tempted to brighten up a dull interview or speech story by changing the reporter's indirect quotations to direct ones. He must not do it. A direct quotation may be changed to a paraphrase, but when the desk changes a paraphase to a direct quotation it is putting words in the speaker's mouth.

If you want to, change this:

```
     "You're a bum," Houndstooth shouted at
Miasma.
```

to this:

```
     Houndstooth called Miasma a nasty name.
```

But don't change this:

```
     Houndstooth called Miasma a nasty name.
```

to this:

```
     "You're a nasty name," Houndstooth shouted
at Miasma.
```

Attribution

No one will object if your newspaper notes on its own authority that there are four seasons, that water is essential to life, or that World War II ended in 1945.

But if it reports without noting authority or source that Democrats are more sensible than Republicans, that Smith was to blame for the traffic crash involving Jones, or that Shakespeare was a pseudonym for Bacon, you may have an argument on your hands.

The copyreader must know when, as well as what, to quote. And if he is to use this knowledge effectively, he must know how to quote. That means he must know the style and language of "attribution," the identification of the source of a statement or information.

In general, unless the reporter is recording his own first-hand observations, he must cite the authority for his material. (Who *says* that Democrats are more sensible than Republicans? Who *says* Smith went through a red light? Who *says* he has new information on the Baconian theory?)

The principle is simple enough, and most reporters understand it. The problem lies in its application. It's easy for a reporter, close to a story, to report as fact something that he has only been told is fact, or that he only believes is fact. He can also easily slip into an essay style of writing, inadvertently omitting attribution and thus, by implication, setting himself up as an expert when he is not. This is a hazard especially in reporting a speech, for it takes skill to attribute all the words to the speaker yet keep the attribution from becoming monotonous and intrusive.

That is not to say that the obituary writer who has not personally checked for a heartbeat must give authority for the fact of death, or that the police reporter who has not watched the handcuffs snapped on must give the authority for the fact of an arrest, or that an announcement of a meeting of the International Students Club must quote the president as saying it will begin at 8 p.m.

But a report on the *cause* of death may require attribution to an authority, particularly if legal questions are involved; the circumstances of an arrest often cannot be reported fairly and accurately without attribution to a police agency; and a report that a club meeting will include an effort to impeach the president may require that a dissident club member be quoted.

What can happen when a story isn't properly attributed and qualified is illustrated by this lead from a metropolitan newspaper:

> In the view of hundreds of persons who stood by, a 28-year-old man was repeatedly stabbed yesterday by a burly Negro who tried to force his attentions on the victim's attractive red-haired wife in Times Square.

The next day the paper carried a story that began this way:

> Mrs. Sandra Saia, 24, an attractive redhead, was charged last night with obstructing justice by telling cops that a burly Negro masher had stabbed her husband in Times Square Sunday afternoon. Before being booked, she admitted that the assailant was an ex-boyfriend but refused to identify him, police said.

There's no handy rule that can give foolproof guidance on citing a source. The reporter and the editor must use judgment. But, in general, attribution to authority is essential when events or the situation may be or can be disputed. Attribution may be skipped when the facts are self-evident, recognized as true historically, clearly not subject to dispute, or of a commonplace and noncontroversial nature.

Having made the decision to cite a source, the reporter must frame the attribution carefully. Sloppy handling can mean ambiguity, clutter, and awkward construction.

Here are a few general principles that are frequently ignored:

(1) A direct quotation should be fastened grammatically to the speaker, not loosely associated with him by implication.

Don't say: Prof. Inkwater was pessimistic. "You are going to cause an explosion and kill us all."

Make it: Prof. Inkwater was pessimistic. "You are going to cause an explosion and kill us all," he said.

(2) A continuous quotation should be attributed only once.

Don't say: "We were robbed," the coach said. "The officials ruined us with imbecilic calls," he continued. "Don't quote me," he added.

Make it: "We were robbed," the coach said. "The officials ruined us with imbecilic calls. Don't quote me."

(3) When two or more sentences of direct quotation run continuously, the speaker should be identified in the first sentence.

Don't say: "This is a democracy, and the majority rules. If we adults don't practice what we preach, we can't expect the younger generation to listen to us. I will leave this matter to the students. If they want to burn down the gymnasium, they may do so," Dean Longsuffer said.

Make it: "This is a democracy, and the majority rules," Dean Longsuffer said. "If we adults don't practice what we preach, we can't expect the younger generation to listen to us. I will leave this matter to the students. If they want to burn down the gymnasium, they may do so."

Or: "This is a democracy," Dean Longsuffer said, "and the majority rules. If we adults. . . ."

Or: Dean Longsuffer said: "This is a democracy, and the majority rules. If we adults. . . ."

(4) To avoid awkward construction (like a jarring shift from the third to the first person), fragmentary quotations and complete quotations should be separated rather than run together as one.

Don't say: He admitted that he "got pretty uptight when the gymnasium was burned. I didn't like it one bit."

Make it: He admitted that he "got pretty uptight" when the gymnasium was burned. "I didn't like it one bit," he said.

Or: He admitted that he "got pretty uptight when the gymnasium was burned," adding: "I didn't like it one bit."

Or: He admitted that he was upset by the destruction of the gymnasium. "I didn't like it one bit," he said.

Editing to correct slips in attribution can be fairly simple. For example, note the four basic faults that appear in this story:

Peter Popover, British Empire heavyweight champion, retired from the ring today after suffering a 13-second knockout in his American debut.

Popover was counted out after being hit once by George (Tiger) Cubb, unranked Rhode Island light-heavyweight, in a bout at Madison Square Garden last night.

"That punch convinced me," Popover said at a champagne breakfast in his motel suite this morning. "I outweighed the little Yank five stone and should have been able to trade blows with him," he added.

Popover said he isn't interested in a return bout. "I didn't see the blighter this time, so there's small point in having another go at him."

The personable Briton said he was hit by "an overhand right traveling at express-train speed. It struck me with sledgehammer force."

Cubb viewed the bout differently. "I hadn't hardly realized the fight had started. I tapped him on the nose with a left jab and he toppled over on his back. Then he just laid there like he was dead," he said.

Cubb said he doesn't care to fight Popover again. "I need more exercise."

Popover's manager, Sir Richard J. Daley-Gargle, expressed surprise at his fighter's retirement. Popover had said "nothing whatever to him about it," Sir Richard told reporters.

Now see how easy it is to correct them:

Peter Popover, British Empire heavyweight champion, retired from the ring today after suffering a 13-second knockout in his American debut.

Popover was counted out after being hit once by George (Tiger) Cubb, unranked Rhode Island light-heavyweight, in a bout at Madison Square Garden last night.

"That punch convinced me," Popover said at a champagne breakfast in his motel suite this morning. "I outweighed the little Yank five stone and should have been able to trade blows with him." ~~he added.~~

Popover said he isn't interested in a return bout. "I didn't see the blighter this time," he said, "so there's small point in having another go at him."

The personable Briton said he was hit by "an overhand right traveling at express-train speed."

He added: "It struck me with sledgehammer force."

Cubb viewed the bout differently. "I hadn't hardly realized the fight had started," he said. "I tapped him on the nose with a left jab and he toppled over on his back. Then he just laid there like he was dead." ~~he said.~~

Cubb said he doesn't care to fight Popover again. "I need more exercise," he commented.

Popover's manager, Sir Richard J. Daley-Gargle, expressed surprise at his fighter's retirement. Popover had said "nothing whatever to ~~him~~ me about it," Sir Richard told reporters.

Verbs of attribution are hurdles that some reporters can't clear cleanly, or at all.

The copy editor must remember, first, that the attributive verb is supposed to describe the act of using lips, tongue, vocal cords, and other physiological equipment to speak. This fact is hard to reconcile with the following passages:

> "I simply don't know the answer," he frowned.
>
> "I'm a doctor, lawyer, minister, teacher and emergency squad member all rolled into one," he grinned.
>
> "Excuse me," he coughed.

It's as hard to frown, smile, and cough words as it is to hear a rose, smell a concerto, taste a drumbeat, feel a sunrise, or see a toothache. If the reporter has mislaid his senses, the copyreader should bring him to them.

Verbs that describe the way words are spoken are almost as troublesome. These are verbs such as hiss, sigh, snap, snort, groan, bark, shout, mumble, whisper, and cry. The copyreader should make sure they are properly used. People don't hiss "Hello" or bark "Would you like to go to the movies tonight?" or groan "Have another piece of cheese, if you care to."

As for the more ordinary verbs of attribution—the ones that crop up repeatedly in routine news stories—any reader knows that a news source can

charge, declare, affirm, relate,
recall, aver, reiterate,
allege, conclude, explain, point out,
answer, note, retort or shout,
rejoin, demand, repeat, reply,
ask, expostulate or sigh,
blurt, suggest, report or mumble,
add, shoot back, burst out or grumble,
whisper, call, assert or state,
vouchsafe, cry, asseverate,
snort, recount, agree, opine,
whimper, simper, wheedle, whine,
mutter, murmur, bellow, bray,
whinny, or . . . let's see now . . .
SAY!

The point of this doggerel is that "say" is a neutral word that connotes only the utterance of words. It tells nothing of the way in which words are spoken, the circumstances of the utterance, or the attitude of the person being quoted. It's a colorless word. But while it doesn't brighten a passage, neither does it call attention to itself. Unlike more descriptive verbs, it can be used repeatedly without becoming a nuisance.

Most other verbs of attribution connote something beyond the simple fact of speaking. They aren't to be scorned on this account. On the contrary, they should be treated with more respect than they usually command.

"Point out" and "note"—two favorites of reporters seeking variety—both mean to call attention to a matter of fact. Thus a paper is safe in having a speaker "note" that Democrats have held the White House for about as many years as Republicans in the 20th Century, but if it lets him "note" that Democrats are more deserving than Republicans it is being partisan.

Among other frequently used and misused attributive verbs are "add," "declare," "state," "assert," "relate," "exclaim," and "explain."

"Add" can be useful, but the word often connotes an afterthought, a comment of somewhat less importance than what has gone before. So it can be misleading, or even absurd, as it is here:

> He said that he regretted being late for the meeting, but that his tardiness was unavoidable. "I fell out of an airplane on the way," he added.

"Declare," "state," and "assert" all connote a certain formality of delivery. "Declare" has an added connotation of forthrightness or openness, "state" of positiveness, and "assert" of positive, strong, or plain speaking.

"Relate" means to give an account or report, and like the verbs just discussed it conveys a sense of formality.

One who "exclaims" is not just saying something; he is crying out in sudden emotion.

"Explain" is much abused. Reporters often use it as a neutral synonym for "say," but because it means "to make plain" or "to make understandable" it is editorial if used this way:

> "It was my husband's fault," she explained.

Or this way:

> "There were no space satellites in the 19th century," he explained.

In the first example, the verb implies that the lady was telling the truth, and so the paper seems to be on her side. In the second, the verb implies that the speaker was addressing an audience of dolts.

The copyreader should prevent the reporter from seeming to read minds rather than report what he has heard. The newsman usually knows only what the speaker said, not what he feels, believes, thinks, hopes, or expects of the future. So the copyreader must often change verbs of feeling, believing, thinking, hoping, and expecting to verbs of saying, commenting, and predicting.

Greater license and informality are permissible in interpretive analysis, the interview story, and the personality feature. Here the reader can assume that the writer has spent some time with the news source, or studying his conduct, and is qualified to interpret his attitude and state of mind.

Because it must pin virtually every sentence on a source, the speech story presents one of the most difficult attribution problems. The writer who cannot vary his sentence pattern may set up a monotonous drumbeat of "he said" sentences. In an effort to break the pattern, he may turn to stilted or inaccurate verbs. Or he may decide that he doesn't have to attribute everything after all, and come up with a mixture of attributed and unattributed statements. The copyreader must help out, but he must use care. Here's a passage that falls into a monotonous drumbeat category:

> He said that he disagrees with the common belief that "television is making the world more actual to those who view it." He said that he does not believe that people are getting objective news. He said that he thinks television men strive to find drama in news stories and produce programs which resemble television dramas. He said that he thinks coverage of the Vietnam war looks something like a "Man from UNCLE" episode. He noted that newsmen were making a legend of Martin Luther King Jr. through dramatic coverage of events following his death.

The copyreader who handled the passage was properly disturbed by its monotony. But he didn't help it much, because in his changes he violated a couple of other principles: he put the paper in the position of reporting what the speaker believed, rather than what he said, and he made the last two sentences read like statements of fact rather than the speaker's opinion. Here is his edited version:

> He said that he disagrees with the common belief that television "is making the world more actual to those who view it." He believes that people are not getting objective news. Television men, he said, strive to find drama in news stories and produce programs which resemble television dramas. Coverage of the Vietnam war looks like something from a "Man from UNCLE" episode. Newsmen are making a legend of Martin Luther King Jr. through dramatic coverage of events following his death.

With a little more care, he might have produced this:

> He charged that television news is not objective, and that it blurs the viewer's concept of reality. Television newsmen, he said, try to emulate television dramatists, with the result that war films resemble episodes from "Man from UNCLE" and coverage of spectacular crimes like the assassination of Martin Luther King Jr. makes the principals legends instead of men.

Underattribution can change a news report into an essay. Here's an example from a story on a speech:

> With all her power, size, population and rapid growth, China's greatest weakness is still her inability to feed and sustain her population. Besides that, Peking is very paranoid. She sees herself as surrounded by enemies. That she is, says Mr. Salisbury, but the paranoia is that she thinks the enemy is united against her. This compounds the problem in Vietnam.

Only one of the five statements in this paragraph is attributed to a source. Even that one is mishandled, for it is reported not as what Mr. Salisbury said on one occasion but as what he "says" all the time. Could be he does, but the reporter's assignment was one speech, not a general philosophy. The copyreader could have helped the paragraph this way:

> *Salisbury said that despite* ~~With all~~ her power~~, size, population~~ and rapid growth, China~~'s greatest weakness is still her inability~~ *is unable* to feed ~~and sustain~~ her population, *and suffers from a* ~~Besides that, Peking is very~~ "paranoid" *fear that* ~~She sees herself as~~ *she is* surrounded by enemies, *who are* ~~That she is, says Mr. Salisbury, but the paranoia is that she thinks the enemy is~~ united against her. This *fear* compounds the problem in Vietnam, *he said.*

Good organization, varied sentence structure, and skillful use of direct quotation combined with paraphrase are the best ways to prevent monotony of attribution.

One device is to group allied comments and hang them on one verb of attribution, as in:

> He made these points:
>
> He gave this account:
>
> He said this is impractical because . . .
>
> Police said it happened this way:

Another is to use several sentences of direct quotation continuously.

Another is to substitute a description of content for direct or indirect quotation, as in: "He told how he had prayed for strength as he fought to bring the boat through the storm."

And another is to approach the subject matter in different ways, as illustrated by these excerpts:

> Robert Eaton, youthful skipper of the Quaker yacht Phoenix, told a small audience on the University campus last night that. . .

He cited a Buddhist priest's charge that. . .

Speaking briefly on the mission of the Phoenix, Eaton said that. . .

He emphasized that. . .

Most of Eaton's talk was a denunciation of. . .

He said this country has. . .

As examples, he cited American involvement in. . .

Eaton said that. . .

Nevertheless, he said '. . .

He described the effects of. . .

Noting the President's most recent effort to. . .

Eaton said that. . .

The United States, he added, would not. . .

Although attribution seems generally easier to handle in the interview story than in the speech story, one of the most irritating of all bad habits crops up most frequently in the interview. Here are examples:

When asked about the requirements of a radio announcer, James said that "radio work is a job which requires mental and physical dexterity combined with wit, initiative and a good radio voice."

When asked what she learned from the ordeal, she said, "I learned how alone you really are."

When asked how the war there could best be won, the major said that the U.S. would have to put forth a maximum of effort in order to overcome the Vietcong.

When asked how he was notified of a fire, Mr. Weeks explained that there were three methods used by his department.

Asked if she had encountered any problems in advising the girls, Miss Dudt replied that she had been afraid the girls would not come to her.

What's irritating about these passages is that they are wordy: the introductory questions are superfluous. Now take a look at them, edited, and note that here they say the same thing in half as many words:

~~When asked about the requirements of a radio announcer,~~ James said that ~~"radio work is a job which~~ being an announcer "requires mental and physical dexterity combined with wit, initiative and a good radio voice."

~~When asked what she learned~~ from the ordeal, she said, ~~"I~~ she learned "how alone you really are."

~~When asked how the war there could best be won,~~ the major said that to overcome the Vietcong and win the war, the U.S. would have to put forth a maximum ~~of~~ effort. ~~in order to overcome the Vietcong.~~

~~When asked how he was notified of a fire,~~ Mr. Weeks ~~explained that~~ said there ~~were~~ are three ~~methods used by~~ ways to notify his department of a fire.

~~Asked if she had encountered any problems in advising the girls,~~ Miss Dudt (said) ~~replied~~ that (before) she (began advising, she) had been afraid the girls would not come to her.

This is the way it is, most of the time. The question is almost always implicit in the answer, and it's only the answer that is of any concern to the reader.

There are times when there's a reason to report on the questioning. It may be the most convenient way to show the relevance of a direct quotation. You may want to show that a politician or a businessman or a labor leader or someone else in the public eye didn't volunteer anything, or that the information he gave was dragged out of him. The nature of the questioning then is relevant. For dramatic effect, or for humor, or to provide a transcript as a matter of record, you may want to handle a story in a "Q and A" fashion. Then, too, the questioning is relevant.

But if the question adds nothing to the story but length, kill it.

Grammar

THE copyreader need not know how to parse a sentence, decline a noun, or define a gerundive phrase, but he must recognize bad grammar when he sees it. He must correct the verb that disagrees with its subject, the pronoun that disagrees with its antecedent, the participle that dangles, the adverbial clause that wanders, and the preposition that wears conjunction's clothing.

Some errors are more common than others. The collective noun, for example, should always be a warning of grammatical peril. Collective nouns represent groups of things taken as a whole—teams, clubs, schools, departments, associations, agencies. Along with the verbs and pronouns associated with them, they must be treated as singular.

Here are some typical miscues:

> The jury of seven men and five women returned <u>their</u> verdict at 3 p.m.
>
> He said the Student Senate did a good job last year when <u>they</u> called a constitutional convention.
>
> The Psychology Department, he charged, is afraid that <u>they</u> would be giving unfair advantage to some students.

Each of these statements calls for a group, or collective, term.

With some collectives, though, good grammar means awkward construction, and the copyreader may want to avoid trouble by recasting a sentence. It sounds pretty pretentious to write "The couple *was* married in 1918." On the other hand, it is ungrammatical to write "The couple *were* married in 1918." Possible solutions: "*They* were married in 1918" or "Mr. and Mrs. Watt were married in 1918."

Disagreement in number is common in other contexts, too. In an inverted sentence in which the verb precedes the subject, it can be relatively hard to spot. For example:

> Included in his plans is a letter to the governor, a campaign to make the Clerical Service print material for the group, and a Thanksgiving dinner for retired people in the area.

Since the subject is plural, the verb should be, too.

Disagreement or inconsistency may result when the reporter can't decide whether he is writing about one person or several. Consider the role of one meal pass if the following passage is taken literally:

> Women who checked out of the University residence halls last weekend and let someone else use their meal pass didn't have a meal pass when they got back to school.

The copyreader should make the sentence consistently singular or consistently plural. Two possibilities:

> A woman who checked out of a University residence hall last weekend and let someone else use her meal pass didn't have a pass when she got back to school.

> Women who checked out of University residence halls last weekend and let others use their meal passes didn't have passes when they got back to school.

Pronouns must be watched for a number of errors besides inconsistency. One is the missing antecedent. Because it replaces a noun and has no independent meaning, the pronoun must be linked grammatically to the noun it replaces. Consider these sentences:

> The chief defense lawyer, Thomas Gaumer, said they are planning an appeal to the Superior Court.

> These impressions go to proofreaders who mark mistakes and send it to an operator.

If the first passage stands alone, the pronoun "they" is meaningless. The only noun it can grammatically refer to is lawyer Gaumer, and Gaumer, presumably, is one person—a "he," and not a "they." The copyreader has options here. He can change "they are" to "he is," "he and his client are," "the defense is," or "defense lawyers are."

The second passage is meaningless because the pronoun "it" must refer to impressions or mistakes, and neither reference makes sense. The copyreader should get rid of the pronoun and replace it with a noun. In this case, the word he wants is "proofs."

Usually, a pronoun should refer to a specific noun rather than to a general idea embodied in a phrase or clause. Take this sentence:

> The Faculty Council voted not to accept the bowl bid, which drew the fire of the downtown press and several influential alumni groups.

The problem here is not so much grammar as clarity. While the reporter meant to say that the Faculty Council's action aroused opposition, what he actually said was that the press and alumni groups opposed the bowl bid. The copyreader might make this change:

> The Faculty Council's (vote against accepting) ~~voted not to accept~~ the bowl bid, ~~which~~ drew the fire of the downtown press and several influential alumni groups.

The drifting "which" just illustrated is one of the most troublesome of the disconnected, floating clauses. Here are two more examples of it:

> Members felt it would be a way to generate good feelings in the community and to help people, which some members feel should be one of the organization's main concerns.

> The reserve fund covers extra expenses of organizations which weren't included in their original budgets.

Here is what the copyreader could do with them:

> Members felt it would be a way to generate
> good feelings in the community and ~~to help~~ do
> ~~people, which~~ (what) some ~~members~~ feel should be
> ~~one of the organization's main concerns.~~ a principal activity: help people.

> The reserve fund covers extra expenses
> ~~of organizations~~ which weren't included in
> ~~their~~ the organizations' original budgets.

The "case" of a pronoun (whether it is the subject or the object: he or him, she or her, they or them, who or whom, etc.) causes more trouble than it should. Few reporters would write "Him gave a speech" or "The car struck she," but many make the identical mistake when the sentence structure muffles the "sound" of the pronoun. "Who" and "whom" are particularly troublesome. Here is a sentence, filed by a wire service, which was carried without change by several daily newspapers:

> A ground and air search continued for the other 11, <u>whom</u> Warden E.C. Ellsworth Jr. said forced their way out of a rear window of a prison farm dormitory in the pre-dawn hours Monday.

In this passage, the pronoun is the subject of the verb "forced," not the object of the verb "said," and should therefore be the nominative "who," not the objective "whom." The story might just as well say, "Them forced their way out of a rear window."

Sometimes a writer tries to improve the sound by corrupting the pronoun into the intensive or reflexive form (himself, herself, myself, etc.), as in this passage:

> He said John Evers, the other assistant trainer, and himself carry out their duties pretty much on their own.

It would be absurd to write, "He said himself carries out his duties pretty much on his own," and it doesn't lessen the absurdity to add the name of the other assistant. The copyreader could do this:

> `He said (he and) John Evers, the other`
>
> `assistant trainer, ~~and himself~~ carry`
>
> `out their duties pretty much on their own.`

Verbs rank second only to pronouns as grammatical troublemakers in the newsroom. And like pronouns they are most temperamental in matters of agreement and consistency. The copyreader must make sure they agree with their subjects in number, and should watch for inconsistencies in tense and mood.

As far as tense is concerned, note the difference in meaning here:

(a) He told the judge he was drinking.
(b) He told the judge he had been drinking.

While (b) indicates that the man was telling about an activity that he had engaged in at some previous time, (a) indicates that he was having a nip during the proceedings in court.

And note the flaw in this sentence:

> `The punter was knocked flat on his back,`
>
> `Coach Buhldozier said after the game, and a`
>
> `penalty for roughing the kicker should be imposed.`

Obviously, it's too late for the imposition of a penalty. The copyreader should do this:

> `The punter was knocked flat on his back,`
>
> `Coach Buhldozier said after the game, and a`
>
> `penalty for roughing the kicker should ~~be~~ (have been) imposed.`

The desk should also be alert to shifts from the indicative to the subjunctive mood. It happens all the time, like this:

> Either organ music <u>will be provided</u> all day in the cafeteria of the Student Union, she reported, or a group <u>would sing</u> Christmas carols at meals.

> He predicted that the Tigers would win if they can avoid injuries during the last week of practice.

The first example should be edited to read either "would be provided" or "will sing." The second should read either "will win" or "could avoid."

Thanks largely to television commercials, the distinction between the preposition "like" and the conjunctions "as" and "as if" or "as though" is badly blurred in many minds. The distinction remains, however, and sentences such as these are grammatical horrors:

> She was late, like everyone expected.

> He acted like he owned the store.

A corollary horror is the substitution of "as" for "like" or "such as":

> He urged greater student support for traditional activities as Homecoming, Singing on the Steps, May Week and Class Day.

The copyreader should deal ruthlessly with these passages:

> She was late, ~~like~~ as everyone expected.

> He acted ~~like~~ as if he owned the store.

> He urged greater student support for traditional activities ~~as~~ like Homecoming, Singing on the Steps, May Week and Class Day.

Other grammatical villains that lurk about the newsroom are dangling participles and gerund phrases, straying adverbial clauses and other modifiers, faulty parallelisms, and misplaced conjunctions. Remember that it is as much a word's function as its place in a sentence that makes its usage precise or imprecise. Here are some examples, with suggested corrections:

> Obviously surprising Nee and Radford, the plan was attacked by many parents.

The participle "surprising" seems to modify "plan." It's a dangler because what surprised the men was the attack, not the plan. Make it:

To the obvious surprise of

~~Obviously surprising~~ Nee and Radford,

the plan was attacked by many parents.

* * *

He said he first became interested

when he read about a lodge meeting inviting

all to come.

"Inviting" is a dangler because the only word it can modify is "meeting," and that doesn't make sense. So make it:

He said he ~~first~~ became interested

an open invitation to

when he read ~~about~~ a lodge meeting. ~~inviting~~

~~all to come.~~

* * *

Having had penicillin shots many

times before, a doctor gives a student a

penicillin shot at the infirmary.

The dangling participle makes it seem that the doctor is getting revenge. Make it:

Having had penicillin shots many

gets another

times before, ~~a doctor gives~~ a student

from a doctor

~~penicillin shot~~ at the infirmary.

* * *

Are you tired, low, have that

rundown feeling, or just plain sick?

Or are you have that wonderful feeling that all's right with the world? Parallel construction is needed here. Make it:

feeling

Are you tired, low, ~~have that~~

rundown, ~~feeling,~~ or just plain sick?

* * *

```
    Passing a staff member in the hallway,
she may not know the student's name.
```

The dangling participle leaves the reader hopelessly confused about who is passing whom, and who knows whose name. Make it:

```
    Passing A staff member (Passing) in the hallway,
she may not know the student's name.
```

• • •

```
    By taking away this privilege, these
students and others could be deprived of a
college education,
```

The dangling gerund phrase puts the students in the position of depriving themselves. Make it:

```
    By (losing) taking away this privilege, these
students and others could be deprived of a
college education.
```

• • •

```
    By having all the students
together, an early breakfast can be
served.
```

This dangling gerund phrase, like the one before it, has nothing to cling to. Make it:

```
    By having all the students
together, (the school can serve) an early breakfast. can be
served.
```

• • •

Hall said the public image of the University would improve by offering the continuing education service.

Quite an active image. It's a dangling gerund phrase again. Make it:

Hall said the [university would improve its] public image ~~of the University would improve~~ by offering the continuing education service.

* * *

Without knowing the text of St. Matthew, the movie would have made no sense at all.

This says the movie knew the text of St. Matthew. It's another dangling gerund phrase. Make it:

[If the viewer had not known] ~~Without knowing~~ the text of St. Matthew, the movie would have made no sense at all.

* * *

Miss Grauman indicated that, if successful, credit for the courses might be given in future years.

The dangling phrase ascribes the potential success to the credit, not, as intended, to the courses. Make it:

Miss Grauman indicated that, if [the courses are] successful, credit ~~for the courses~~ [may] ~~might~~ be given in future years.

* * *

Can this nation afford to fight both

a major war in Vietnam and at the same time

attend to crucial problems at home and

abroad?

The misplaced correlative conjunction doesn't cause ambiguity. It's just bad grammar. The correlatives—both-and, either-or, neither-nor, not only-but also—must be followed by parallel constructions. The above sentence should read:

Can this nation afford (both) to fight ~~both~~

a major war in Vietnam and (to) ~~at the same time~~

attend to crucial problems at home and

abroad?

* * *

She said she only attended the rally

because her fiance wanted to go.

A misplaced "only," one of the most common of the misplaced modifiers, should be relocated so:

She said she ~~only~~ attended the rally (only)

because her fiance wanted to go.

* * *

He will transfer to the

University in the spring, where he

will be a leading candidate for one

of the linebacker spots next fall.

This misplaced adverbial clause changes spring from a season to a place. Make it:

In the spring
He will transfer to the
University, ~~in the spring,~~ where he
will be a leading candidate for one
of the linebacker spots next fall.

* * *

He and other members of the squad
will report in mid-August to the Spinners
Lake training camp, when conditioning
for the fall campaign will begin in earnest.

Same problem, this time making a camp a time instead of a place. Make it:

He and other members of the squad
will report ~~in mid-August~~ to the Spinners
Lake training camp (in mid-August,) when conditioning
for the fall campaign will begin in earnest.

The most common punctuation problem is the comma splice, or comma fault. This is using a comma to separate sentences, or to replace a conjunction between the elements of a compound sentence. Here are some typical examples:

The American section is composed of
58 cities, among them are Las Vegas, Reno,
Salt Lake City, Denver, Dallas, Montgomery,
Atlanta and Miami.

The fault comes after "cities." The copyreader should delete "are," or change the comma to a period, or let the comma stand but make it read "among which are."

```
    The boys plan to use an old school bus fixed
up like a camper for their transportation, their
musical equipment valued at over $5,000 will be
carried in a trailer.
```

The fault comes after "transportation." The copyreader should change the comma to a period, or let the comma stand and make it read "and to carry their musical equipment, valued at over $5,000, in a trailer."

```
    Drug use, she continued, may be considered
in the same category as drinking, a few girls
do it and this makes many think that all do it.
```

The fault comes after "drinking." The copyreader should change the comma to a colon or a dash, or he should change the comma to a period and write in an attribution in the next sentence.

Most newspapers drop the comma before the final "and" in a list, like this:

```
    Williams, Roberts, Fredericks and
Peters were appointed to the committee.
```

Sometimes reporters don't understand this rule, or misinterpret it, with the result that they punctuate descriptive material this way:

```
    Donald Keith, 58 and Charles Hood, 41,
spotted the wreckage.
```

Or they make a mistake like this:

```
    He is survived by his sons John, of
Harrisburg and Edward, of Philadelphia.
```

Obviously, the copyreader should insert commas after "58," "sons," and "Harrisburg."

Faulty punctuation sometimes causes trouble in the use of titles. When a title precedes a name and is used as a title, not a description, there should be no punctuation:

```
Arts College Dean Robert Coonrod
```

But when the title is used as description, or an appositive, it is separated from the name by a comma:

```
The dean of the Arts College, Robert Coonrod
```

Reporters sometimes combine the two forms, producing this improper construction:

```
Arts College Dean, Robert Coonrod
```

The copyreader may either delete the comma or write in "the."

By convention, quotation marks always go outside the comma and the period, as in:

```
     She liked to listen to "Tiptoe Through the
Tulips," but didn't care for "Yellow Rose
of Texas."
```

It sometimes seems to be an illogical convention, so watch for violations.

The Use and Abuse of Language

Most people abuse the language once in a while, and it is argued that reporters are people. Hence, the copyreader must sometimes deal with writing that is complex, overblown, trite, ambiguous, redundant, or garbled. He must be cautious when making changes for clarity, for he must be sure he understands what the reporter means. Often he must track down the reporter and ask him. Sometimes he hasn't time and sometimes the reporter is untrackable, or isn't sure what he means, or is uncooperaive.

So there are limits to what the copyreader can do. He may have to delete an unclear passage, or let it go as is on the theory that at least a few readers will understand. But, within the limits imposed by circumstance, he should do what he can to brighten and clarify.

The editor must remember, first of all, that the newspaper is written for a mass audience. Stories should not be "written down" on this account, but they should recognize that even the best-educated reader is not a specialist in everything. The copyreader should therefore get rid of specialized terms that may not be generally understood, or if they are essential to the story he should make sure they are explained.

A courthouse reporter may write that a summons in trespass has been filed with the court clerk, that a defendant has pleaded *nolo contendere*, or that a judge has issued a writ of *mandamus* or a writ of *certiorari*. The copyreader should change the summons in trespass to a suit for damages, the plea of *nolo contendere* to a plea of no defense, the writ of *mandamus* to an order compelling a public official to take some sort of action, and the writ of *certiorari* to a decision to review the ruling of a lower court. From a legal standpoint the technical language is more accurate, but such technical accuracy may not be needed in a news story.

Similarly, the copyreader handling a story with medical terms may want to change "fractured tibia" to "broken leg" or "inflammation of the duodenum" to "inflammation of the intestine." If these terms seem too general, he may want to use "tibia" and "duodenum" but explain that the tibia is the shinbone and that the duodenum is the uppermost section of the small intestine.

The story's position in the paper may affect the way the vocabulary is handled. On the sports page, it would be ridiculous to explain "blitz," "free safety," or "stunting defense," but a woman's page interview with a pro football player's wife might well include a translation of such terms. Similarly, terms like "futures," "short selling" and "margin requirements" could stand alone on the financial page but might be explained in a story carried run-of-paper.

In general, the copyreader should seek the greatest simplicity consistent with precise meaning. The goal is readability as well as clarity. It is easier to shout "fire" than "conflagration," and the shorter, simpler word is usually easier to read, too. Thus most editors prefer "cuts" to "lacerations," "bruises" to "contusions," "use" to "utilize," "about" to "approximately," and "bought" to "purchased." When meaning requires it, of course, the longer word should stand. If an accident victim has suffered a laceration of the brain, it would be silly to change the word to "cut."

The simplicity and directness of news writing should preclude euphemisms. There is seldom any reason to substitute "pass away" for "die," "under the influence of liquor" for "drunk," or "criminal assault" for "rape." And there can be good reasons not to. Unless an assault is military or verbal, for example, it is criminal by nature, and to use "criminal assault" as a substitute for "rape" is to rape the language. An even greater absurdity is to report that a woman killed by bullets, multiple stab wounds, and strangulation has not been "molested."

A relative of the euphemism is the elongation, or multiword synonym. This is a device some writers use to avoid repeating a word, and it is easy to catch because of its contrived sound. The elongator may write about the briny deep, the precious red fluid, the nocturnal resting place, the furry sphere, the long-necked ruminant, the helmeted minion of the law, and the bushy-tailed rodent. The copyreader should see to it that the story tells about the ocean, blood, a bed, a tennis ball, a giraffe, a policeman, and a squirrel.

Reporters can get pretty pretentious by themselves, without help from the professionals in other fields. No copy editor should pass the expression "claimed the life of." (It means *killed.*) And he should remember that words that are hard to pronounce are usually hard to read. Many editors therefore prefer "nomination for governor" to "gubernatorial nomination." The same editors enjoy seeing dogs nip at the heels of reporters who use "councilmanic," "aldermanic," "solon," "finalization," "upcoming," and "opt."

Pompposity, complexity, and elongation affect sentences and paragraphs as well as words and phrases. Here are some sonorous sentences, followed by suggestions for editing:

He feels that this quality supersedes all others in importance.

He feels that this quality (is the most important) ~~supersedes all others in importance~~.

* * *

In most cases monetary reward is expected in return for nursing services rendered.

Nurses usually expect to be paid

~~In most cases monetary reward is expected in return for nursing services rendered.~~

* * *

Mrs. Ross said that she tries to structure her explanations so that they will fit into a child's individual living space.

Mrs. Ross said ~~that~~ she tries to (explain) ~~structure~~ ~~her explanations so that they will fit into~~ (in terms that the child can understand) ~~a child's individual living space~~.

* * *

He has attained 50 year status on the alumni roles.

He [was graduated 50 years ago] ~~has attained 50 year status on the alumni roles~~.

* * *

The benefit of economic funds gives them an attitude of superiority.

[Wealth makes them snobbish] ~~The benefit of economic funds gives them an attitude of superiority.~~

* * *

The correction bank is the next receptor of the printed word.

[Next the type goes to] the correction bank ~~is the next receptor of the printed word~~.

* * *

It requires rereading for corrective purposes.

It [must be read again for errors] ~~requires rereading for corrective purposes.~~

* * *

He sponsored a bill that would

allow 18-year-olds voting privileges.

He sponsored a bill ~~that would~~ to

allow 18-year-olds ~~voting privileges.~~ to vote.

Here are a couple of complete paragraphs that are tough to wade through, with suggestions for editing:

Project Skyfire is studying the

characteristics of northern Rocky

Mountain lightning storms and dis-

charges and their relationships to

the forest fuels they ignite in order

to determine the possibility of reducing

the number of firesetting lightning charges

through weather modification techniques.

Through the Forest Service hopes to learn

Project Skyfire, ~~is studying the~~

why some lightning storms in the

~~characteristics of~~ northern Rocky

cause fires, while others do not.

Mountains ~~lightning storms and dis-~~

The foresters believe that once they

~~charges and their relationships to~~

know this, they may be able to

~~the forest fuels they ignite in order~~

reduce the number of fires by

~~to determine the possibility of reducing~~

seeding clouds and applying other

~~the number of firesetting lightning charges~~

techniques of modifying the

~~through weather modification techniques.~~

weather.

* * *

Mrs. Christopherson used the example of a growing plant in explaining how the handicapped child benefits from the nursery school experience. A plant cannot survive on water, food, or sun alone, but needs a combination of these factors to become healthy.

Mrs. Christopherson said the ~~used the example~~
~~of a growing plant in explaining how~~
~~the handicapped child benefits from the~~
helps the handicapped child by providing
nursery school experience. ~~A plant cannot~~
a varied environment. She likened the child's
~~survive on water, food, or sun alone, but~~
need to that of a plant that must have
~~needs a combination of these factors to~~
a combination of water, food and sunlight
~~become healthy.~~
to survive.

The original Skyfire paragraph is one sentence of 41 words—too long for easy comprehension. It is full of big words that are not hard to grasp singly but are pretty difficult in combination. The phrase "weather modification techniques" is meteorological jargon for "ways to influence (or change) the weather."

In the nursery school passage, the expression "used the example of a growing plant in explaining how" is in itself a cry for help. It does not tell the reader what Mrs. Christopherson said, but instead outlines her subject matter. Seldom is it necessary to give this kind of blunt explanation of the reason behind a comment. Most quotations, direct and indirect, can stand by themselves.

The changes in these two paragraphs amount to rewriting, but the effort is always justified if the copyreader has enough time. In each case he should retype the paragraph and paste it in place.

Effective writing usually is restrained and avoids the excessive use of modifiers. There is nothing fundamentally wrong with modifiers. The trouble is that many writers use them mindlessly.

When motion picture advertisements describe a film as magnificent or colossal or the most expensive ever made or the most thrilling of the last decade or the most shocking in history, few moviegoers are stirred. Similarly, modifiers used too freely in news writing lose their effect.

One of the most overused words in the language is "interested," as we see here:

Prof. Tannenbaum said that interested

persons may purchase trees between 7 and 10 p.m.

Editing would make it:

Prof. Tannenbaum said ~~that interested~~

~~persons may purchase~~ trees will be sold between 7 and 10 p.m.

Here's another useless modifier, in a feature about a new student union building:

This will afford an opportune
place to congregate.

What does "opportune" add?

Another, from a story about a new science laboratory:

The current is easily regulated
by dials on the machine.

What does "easily" add?

You can find throwaway modifers like those in almost any story. Make sure the adjective adds something before you let a story retain a "proper" procedure, an "active" member, a "necessary" step, an "honest" opinion, "clear" evidence, "sworn" testimony, or an "irrefutable" fact.

Sometimes, as in "sworn testimony," the modifier is redundant as well as useless. Redundancy is common in news writing. If a service club announces a meeting at "12 o'clock noon" or "6:30 p.m. Thursday night," the bored reporter may pass it along that way even though he knows better. The copyreader should make it "noon" and "6:30 p.m. Thursday."

Newspaper styles vary on the use of a time in conjunction with "last night," "this morning," "tonight," and the like. Some insist on "5:30 o'clock this morning," while others prefer the less formal "5:30 this morning." Most newsmen don't face the problem much anymore, though, because in modern newspaper usage the words "yesterday," "today," and "tomorrow" and their variations are all but extinct, having given way to the name of the day of the week. This is unfortunate because the so-called modern news style is unnatural: in the spoken language, it's still "nice out today," not "nice out Wednesday."

At any rate, the copyreader should be on the lookout for redundancies like these:

```
        He was a convicted convict.

        He quoted an eyewitness as saying
   he saw the Williams car go through the
   stop sign.

        Corbin said the reason for the
   invitation was due to recent criticism
   of the Messenger by the Student Senate.

        Invariably, he said, there always
   seem to be last-minute objections.

        The reason was because the plane's
   takeoff was delayed by weather.

        She denied being motivated by
   ulterior motives.
```

Let's edit the passages:

He was a ~~convicted~~ convict.

He quoted an eyewitness as saying ~~he saw~~ the Williams car ~~go~~ went through the stop sign.

Corbin said the ~~reason for the~~ invitation was issued ~~due to~~ because of recent criticism of the Messenger by the Student Senate.

Invariably, he said, there ~~always seem to be~~ are last-minute objections.

The reason was ~~because~~ that the plane's takeoff was delayed by weather.

She denied ~~being motivated by~~ having ulterior motives.

Deadline pressures make newspaper writing peculiarly vulnerable to ambiguity. The reporter writes his story and turns it in immediately. Rarely can he put it aside to reread later, when his critical faculties have been refreshed; he must reread at the time of writing, before his mind has been switched to another track. He thus runs the danger of not "hearing" the wrong word, the misplaced phrase, the sentence that can be read two ways—even though only an hour or so later, when the paper is on the street and he his checking his own stuff, he may clap hand to brow and say, "Ohmigosh, look what *I* did!"

One reason the copyreader has a job is to keep the reporter from having days like that. The deskman hasn't been living with the story from the start. He comes upon it fresh and should be able to spot the troubles that escape the writer's eye.

Take this quotation, for example, from a story about a vocational training program for American Indians:

"There were few adjustment problems
because of the fact that the trainees
were Indians," Dr. Pope said.

Dr. Pope appears to be saying that the trainees adjusted well because of their race, but what he meant was that most of the adjustment problems were caused by factors other than race. The copyreader should have questioned the reporter about it. Had he done so, he might have edited the passage this way:

~~"There were few adjustment problems~~
~~because of~~ The fact that the trainees
were Indians," ~~Dr. Pope said~~ caused few
adjustment problems, Dr. Pope said.

Some other examples of ambiguity:

He said he woke his wife and son
and rushed to the street in their night
clothes.

Must have been an odd sight. Edit this way:

He said he ~~woke~~ awakened his wife and son,
and all three rushed to the street in their night
clothes.

* * *

    She introduced him to the nurses
    on his floor and his roommate.

Smothered by white uniforms, apparently. Edit this way:

    She introduced him to his roommate and the nurses
    on his floor ~~and his roommate~~.

* * *

    Asked if he thought that 18-year-olds
    should drink liquor as well as vote, Sen.
    Anderson said "It's not part of my platform,"
    but personally, he thinks they should.

The senator was not urging teen-agers to drink; he was advocating a lower legal drinking age. Edit this way:

    ~~Asked if he thought that 18-year-olds~~
    ~~should drink liquor as well as vote,~~ Sen.
    Anderson said ~~"It's not part of my platform,"~~
    ~~but personally,~~ he thinks 18-year-olds should be allowed ~~they should~~
    to drink as well as vote.

* * *

    He spoke before a meeting of the
    Taxpayers League.

Does that mean he addressed the league, or that the league meeting began after he spoke? The lesson here: don't use "before" as a synonym for "at" or "to." Edit this way:

    He spoke ~~before~~ at a meeting of the
    Taxpayers League.

* * *

"Upward Bound" involves students who
will be high school juniors or seniors
in a two-summer program.

How's that again? Edit this way:

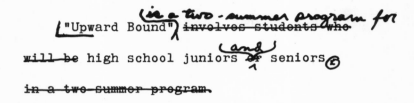

"Upward Bound" is a two-summer program for ~~involves students who~~
~~will be~~ high school juniors and ~~or~~ seniors.
~~in a two-summer program.~~

* * *

Mrs. Halstead believes that the
United States is spoonfeeding democracy
to an unwilling Vietnamese.

Is someone holding his arms? Edit this way:

Mrs. Halstead believes that the
United States is spoonfeeding democracy
to people who do not want it. ~~an unwilling Vietnamese.~~

And just to show, once again, that wire copy isn't necessarily perfect just because it's wire copy:

The law, approved hurriedly by
Congress in response to a rash of
Vietnamese war protests that involved
public destruction of draft cards,
has been declared unconstitutional by
the First U.S. Circuit Court of Appeals.

Some people view them as American protests against the war in Vietnam. Edit this way:

```
    The law, approved hurriedly by
Congress in response to a rash of
~~Vietnamese war~~ protests ~~that involved~~
against the war in Vietnam,
~~public destruction of draft cards,~~
has been declared unconstitutional by
the First U.S. Circuit Court of Appeals.
```

If the language of the news story is sometimes ambiguous, it is also sometimes just plain wrong. The copyreader must watch every word for correct usage. Beginning reporters are particularly likely to make vocabulary mistakes in police coverage. There are a lot of different kinds of thefts and thieves, for example, and while a robbery is a larceny, a larceny is not necessarily a robbery. Similarly, while a murder is a homicide, a homicide is not necessarily a murder. The copyreader should backstop the reporter on his language, and question him if he has any doubt. He should particularly watch out for the use of the words "infer," "hopefully," and "viable." If a news source hints at something, he is implying, not inferring.

There is probably no hope for "hopefully" as a grammatically robust adverb, but even if it makes an independent life for itself, like "luckily" and "predictably," watch out for atrocities like this:

```
    There will be refreshments and
entertainment in the College Inn for
the hopefully defeated Bozeman Spurs.
```

"Viable," a once splendid word, has been ruined by overuse. Although it can mean workable or practicable, its basic meaning is "capable of living" or having the necessary attributes for life. If your writers are throwing a lot of "viable alternatives" and "viable plans" and "viable budgets" at you, try to get some "workables" and "feasibles" and "effectives" in there.

Watch the verbs of attribution and make sure they connote the meanings intended. These passages mean different things:

```
He said his opponents are stupid.
He pointed out that his opponents are stupid.
He explained that his opponents are stupid.
```

Attributive verbs can be appropriate but still misused:

    Several members burst out in
    protest against the suggestion.

This version is less colorful but more idiomatic:

    Several members ~~burst out in~~ shouted
    protest ~~against the suggestion.~~

Watch out for that oddity, the "near" something. The most frequently seen of the breed is the "near riot," but there are also "near tragedies," "near disasters," "near crashes," "near routs," and "near drownings." These nears defy definition as much as a "near fire," a "near storm," or a "near explosion," and as undefinables they should be banished from the newspaper. The editor should be particularly resolute in his duty to preserve the language when a "near" gets averted, as in this absurdity:

    A near tragedy was averted
    Saturday afternoon when a 40-
    year-old Hamilton man, Joe Kochis,
    leaped into an irrigation channel
    and saved a 10-year-old girl from
    drowning.

The copyreader need simply delete "near" to make this lead honest, but to turn it into something really respectable he should do this:

    ~~A near tragedy was averted~~
    ~~Saturday afternoon when~~ A 40-
    year-old Hamilton man, Joe Kochis,
    leaped into an irrigation channel
    and saved a 10-year-old girl from
    drowning, Saturday afternoon.

This editing observes the old principle that the facts can usually speak for themselves. If a child drowns at a picnic, the reader need not be told that the event is sad. A lead like this is trite: "A family outing ended in tragedy yesterday when. . . ."

Watch out for possessives in the use of names: they can change the name if they are misused. The possessive of Hopkins is Hopkins', not Hopkin's.

Beware of words that can be taken either figuratively or literally. This shouldn't get past the copyreader:

The trooper said it was a

miracle that no one was killed.

Without quotation marks around it, "miracle" will be read in its theological sense, and the paper may thus seem to agree that the escape of the persons involved in the crash was an act of God. Make it:

The trooper said it was ~~a~~ surprising

~~miracle~~ that no one was killed.

Be kind to the idiom. A word that is right in one context may be wrong in another. An American speaks of a "traveling salesman," but not of a "traveling berry picker." He speaks of a "migrant berry picker," but not of a "migrant salesman."

Check the ideas in a sentence to be sure that they are consistent with each other. This sentence paints an odd picture: "Contributors will be given a flower." The editor should make it either "Each contributor will get a flower" or "Contributors will get flowers."

Here are assorted other examples of misused language, along with suggestions for editing:

He said that if the Vietnamese

are unwilling to withdraw and to help

rid "the diseases of their own land,

then let them know that we alone can't

save them."

There is an awkward change in point of view here, from third person to direct address, but the chief problem is the misuse of "rid." It's the land, not the disease, that is being referred to.

He said that if the Vietnamese are unwilling to withdraw and ~~to~~ help rid ~~"the diseases of~~ their own land (of disease,) ~~then"~~ (the United States should) let them know that we alone can't save them."

* * *

He praised the value and the importance of the convention.

He's really praising the convention, of course, not its value and importance. Edit it so:

He ~~praised the value and the importance of~~ (said) the convention (,) (is valuable and important).

* * *

She shook her head yes.

An odd thing to do. Fix it like this:

She ~~shook her head yes.~~ (nodded.)

* * *

The girls revealed their ignorance by answering 51.9 per cent of the questions correctly.

Giving the right answers is a funny way to show ignorance. Straighten out the meaning:

The girls ~~revealed their ignorance by answering~~ (answered only) 51.9 per cent of the questions correctly.

* * *

Even the community's animals receive aid from the County Humane Society.

So who else would? Give credit where it's due:

Even the community's animals receive aid ~~from~~ the County Humane Society provides it.

* * *

There will be a question and answer period following the speaker.

Like a faithful old hound dog? Make it:

~~There will be~~ A question and answer period wide follow~~ing~~ the ~~speaker~~ talk.

* * *

Applegate said he will submit next year's suggested lecturers to the council next week.

They must be docile fellows to permit it. Let's be precise:

Applegate said he will submit a list of next year's suggested lecturers to the council next week.

* * *

Warwick said the University required that the tents be erected inside the trees surrounding the Oval.

Squirrels, clear out! Here's what he really said:

Warwick said the University required that the tents be erected inside the (ring of) trees surrounding the Oval.

* * *

Women with 21 privileges have to sign out to participate.

What if they have only 20 privileges? We can mention the age of these women:

Women ~~with~~ (who are) 21 ~~privileges have to~~ (must merely) sign out to participate.

* * *

The demonstrators will begin their 24-hour fast with the noon meal.

You ought to see how they shovel it in when they're *not* fasting! Let's be sensible:

The demonstrators will begin their 24-hour fast ~~with the noon meal.~~ (after breakfast.)

* * *

The reporters and photographers
in Vietnam were not directly smothered
there, she said.

This is ambiguous. The reader can't be sure whether they were smothered indirectly in Vietnam, or shipped out for direct smothering in some other country. Make the intended meaning clear:

The reporters and photographers
in Vietnam were not ~~directly smothered~~ *subject to direct censorship,*
~~there,~~ she said.

* * *

They find themselves in an
affluent society which they cannot enter.

If they are already in it, why should they have to enter it? Their sentiments *can* be expressed:

They find themselves ~~in~~ *at the fringe of* an
affluent society which they cannot enter.

* * *

Generally, he explained, students
are permitted to leave the dormitory
system if they drop out of school.

How liberal can the rulemakers get? Fix it up:

Generally, he explained, students
~~are permitted to leave the dormitory~~
~~system if they~~ *who* drop out of school *are not forced to rejoin the dormitory system when they return.*

* * *

> The object of the study is to discover how living cones have evolved from the petrified cones, Mr. Miller said.

Greater than Columbus' discovery, if they find out! Only a slight change is needed:

> The object of the study is to discover how living cones have evolved from the specimen ~~petrified~~ cones that petrified, Mr. Miller said.

* * *

> He said that the brink between Russia and China is expanding, and that the borders along the Russian-Chinese frontier are lined with heavily armed outposts.

And the hole gets thicker and the water's edge wider, and the trim is lined with chrome. Readers do think, you know. Be exact:

> He said that the rift ~~brink~~ between Russia and China is widening ~~expanding~~, and that the ~~borders along the~~ Russian-Chinese frontier is ~~are~~ lined with heavily armed outposts.

* * *

> "Like it or not, the present Chinese government is here to stay," barked Mansfield.

Arf! Arf! Simplify:

> "Like it or not, the present Chinese government is here to stay," ~~barked~~ Mansfield said.

* * *

```
She swore to herself, "That does it!"
```

And she's from such a nice family, too! Simplify, simplify:

She ~~swore to herself,~~ thought, "That does it!"

* * *

```
The shuffle of feet pounded up the stairs.
```

While the pounding of her heart shuffled in her ears? Let the verb do its own job:

~~The shuffle of~~ Feet pounded up the stairs.

* * *

```
She studied in preparation for a five-week
tour of a living language, the Soviet Union.
```

Italy, on the other hand, must be a dead language. This is the easiest one yet to fix:

She studied Russian in preparation for a five-week tour of ~~a living language,~~ the Soviet Union.

Writing can get even murkier than that, and make no sense at all. As in this passage from a reporter who may think that Ford, General Motors, and Chrysler are the names of states:

```
This is a group of companies including
Washington, Oregon, Utah, Idaho and Montana.
```

Edited:

This is a group of companies ~~including~~ in Washington, Oregon, Utah, Idaho and Montana.

Or this, from a reporter who can't tell the difference between a judge and a decision:

> Criticizing Supreme Court decisions, she said it "coddles the criminal at the expense of law-abiding citizens."

Edited:

> Criticizing (the) Supreme Court ~~decisions,~~ she said it "coddles the criminal at the expense of law-abiding citizens."

Or this, from a reporter who has an odd concept of anatomy:

> She scrubbed each part of her hands and up to three inches above her arms.

Edited:

> She scrubbed ~~each part of~~ her hands and ~~up to three inches above her~~ arms.

Or this, from a reporter who can't tell people from values:

> The Tutor Corps is designed to associate young children with responsible middle class people in hopes that these values will transfer to the child.

Edited:

> (Through) ~~T~~he Tutor Corps ~~is designed to associate young~~ children (get acquainted) with responsible middle class people (and learn about their) ~~in hopes that these~~ values~~ will transfer to the child.~~

Or this, from a reporter who can't distinguish between people and money:

> He said the cost is to be given by 75 per cent of the property owners within the district and 25 per cent by the city.

Edited:

> He said ~~the cost is to be given by 75 per cent of the~~ property owners ~~within~~ in the district ~~and 25~~ will pay 75 per cent ~~by the city.~~ of the cost, and the city 25 per cent.

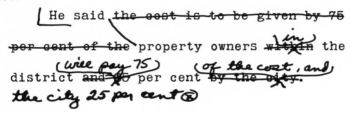

Or this, from a reporter who isn't sure what a date is:

> The date for the debate was set as a Tuesday Topic on Dec. 5 at 4 p.m.

Edited:

> The ~~date for the~~ debate was ~~set as~~ scheduled, a "Tuesday Topic" on Dec. 5 at 4 p.m.

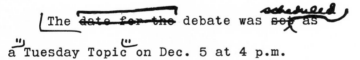

Remember that wire service copy can sometimes be improved, too. Here's a passage, for instance, that forgets that a modifier must have something to modify:

> WASHINGTON — Ninety-year-old Sen. Carl Hayden said Monday he will retire next year after nearly 57 years in Congress, longer than any other man.

Edited:

> WASHINGTON — Ninety-year-old Sen. Carl Hayden said Monday he will retire next year after serving nearly 57 years in Congress, longer than any other man.

The passive voice has its uses, but if a writer leans on it too heavily his writing becomes flabby—lacking the punch that vivid, active verbs supply—and wordy, because it takes longer to say something in the passive than in the active voice. An example:

```
I hate you. (Active)

You are hated by me. (Passive)
```

To cut out the fat, improve the grammar, and make the story clearer and more forceful, sometimes all the copyreader has to do is change the voice, as in these examples:

```
        Selection of the recipient will be

made by the university.
```

~~Selection of the recipient will be~~

~~made by~~ The university will select the recipient.

* * *

```
        Decisions are based on interviews

with the applicant and after evaluating

basic information required of each

applicant.
```

They base their decisions

~~Decisions are based~~ on interviews

~~with the applicant~~ and ~~after evaluating~~

~~basic~~ information supplied by the ~~required of each~~

applicants.

* * *

```
        The students said not enough light

is provided for studying by one desk

lamp and an overhead light bulb.
```

The students said ~~not enough light is provided for studying by~~ one desk lamp and an overhead ~~light~~ bulb, do not provide enough light for studying.

* * *

Several months on the island of Upolu were spent last year by Prof. Barton.

Prof. Barton spent several months on the island of Upolu ~~were spent~~ last year. ~~by Prof. Barton.~~

The overuse of the verb "to be" has the same effect as the overuse of the passive voice. It makes a story flabby. Passages that begin with "there is," "there were," "there will be," and so forth invite quick and easy change:

There will be an installation of officers at a meeting of the Spanish Club Thursday.

~~There will be an installation of officers at a meeting of~~ The Spanish Club will install officers Thursday.

It doesn't take much to improve this type of sentence, either:

Organization of the first girls' flag football team in the state will be Saturday.

~~Organization of~~ The first girls' flag football team in the state will be organized Saturday.

The verb gives a sentence its direction, and should usually appear early. Here it's delayed too long:

> From these invitations, a board comprising Dr. F. D. Anderson, obstetrician; The Rev. Robert Anderson, Congregationalist minister; Gardner Cromwell, law professor; Jack Selway, broadcaster; Elizabeth Johnstone, Welfare Department employee, and Dorothy Simpson, housewife, was formed.

The reader gets lost here because he must plow through the names without knowing their significance. (The sentence might be preparing to say that the board was proposed or was instructed to take some sort of action.) He'll have an easier time if the copyreader will get the key words—"was formed"—up there ahead of the names, either by revamping the first part of the sentence, like this:

> These invitations resulted in the formation of a board composed of Dr. F. D. Anderson . . .

or by making two sentences of it, like this:

> On the basis of responses to these invitations, a board was formed. Members are Dr. F. D. Anderson, obstetrician. . .

The sentence that is too long is like the sentence with the delayed verb. It may be grammatically correct, but it can be hard to follow. The copyreader doesn't have to be a word-counter or a syllable-counter to recognize the sentence that is dragged out. This one is too long:

> Prof. Daniel M. Shonting, who is retiring after 44 years of service in the accounting department, was among 47 members of the faculty and staff honored at the 22nd annual Recognition Dinner given last night in the Ohio Union by the Board of Trustees in tribute to retiring faculty and staff members, as well as current members, who

> have completed 25 or more years of service to the University.

Edited with a period, it would read this way:

> Prof. Daniel M. Shonting, who is retiring after 44 years of service in the accounting department, was among 47 members of the faculty and staff honored at the 22nd annual Recognition Dinner ~~given~~ last night in the Ohio Union~~.~~ ~~by~~ The Board of Trustees (sponsored the event) in tribute to retiring faculty and staff members, as well as current members, who have completed 25 or more years of service to the University.

Original and consistent figures of speech brighten a story, but the trite simile and the mixed metaphor tarnish it. "This is confusing," wrote a college columnist, "when a team is knee-deep in a pennant race." The reader can only wonder whether the contenders were racing through a bog.

A four-paragraph sports story (and where bad figures are being studied it's hard to stay out of the locker room) said that "the basketball mentor was at the helm preparing to launch platoons of cagers into high gear in the season's lid-lifter on the hardwoods, against an unheralded foe." The tired old clichés aren't the only problem here. The metaphors are so badly scrambled that the reader must try to picture a sea captain shoving a bunch of infantrymen down the ways from a saucepan into whirring machinery. The mind boggles.

Sportswriters can't be blamed for all the bollixed figures of speech, though. Here's a casual inconsistency that the copyreader should have caught:

> He was born at the height of the Depression.

That is sort of like saying an astronaut soared to the lowest part of the sky. Obviously, the passage should have been edited to:

> He was born at the ~~height~~ (depth) of the Depression.

No one can deny, of course, that the mixed metaphor produces some interesting combinations:

> Political overtones flavored the meeting.

(May I have a little more arpeggio on my asparagus, please?)

Like figures of speech, hyperbole can be useful, but inadvertent exaggeration can be destructive and the copyreader should be on the lookout for it. In a straightforward advance story about a ski meet, this is out of place:

> Members of the patrol will ski over the area and will be ready to administer first aid the split second there is an accident.

The "split second" is silly exaggeration and should come out.

Obviously this line, from a story about a woman war correspondent, cannot possibly be true:

> She and her husband worked as a team covering all aspects of the war.

The copyreader could make it:

> She and her husband covered the war as a team.

And this, from a story about an outspoken clergyman of controversial views, is also patently false:

> The phone at his home rings constantly with crank calls.

"Constantly" implies regularity. While it might be argued that the reporter did not expect the word to be taken literally, and was simply striving for a general effect, the passage raises a reasonable question: just how much does the phone ring? Sixty times an hour? Twenty times a day? Three times daily between 2 and 6 a.m.? Something specific, even though an estimate, would have far more meaning than the generality. The copyreader can help the reporter if he'll take the trouble to question such generalities.

Flip the coin of meaningless exaggeration and you'll find statements of the obvious. An apocryphal example:

```
      The girl stopped wailing but
   her body shook with sobs.  Tears
   as big as golf balls rolled down
   her cheeks.  She seemed unhappy.
```

And an example from the real world:

```
      Hiring doctors and installing
   the necessary equipment is costly,
   he said, because neither can be
   obtained cheaply.
```

Oh.

Again, from a review of a well-publicized concert by a renowned instrumental group:

```
      All four members of the quartet
   appeared in the concert.
```

Great Scott! The editor's task is simple in all three cases, though: delete everything.

And, finally, among the miscellaneous language problems that reach the copy desk are these five:

The Illogical Participle or Appositive

```
      Receiving a salary of $100 a
   month for his position, Cagle spends
   at least 20 hours a week in the
   treatment room.

      Born in Montgomery, Ala., he is noted
   for the ringing quality of his voice.

      A graduate of Harvard, he
   became interested in the problem
   of overpopulation after a successful
   career in business.

      A member of the First Presbyterian
   Church, Mr. Harriman married the former
   Sarah March of Middletown on June 8, 1935.
```

In none of those passages is there a logical relationship between the first phrase and the second. The editor should separate the ideas, either by recasting the sentences or by giving each thought a sentence of its own.

The Inconsistent Comparison

> Using the old method, it took the street department a week to mix 50 tons of blacktop. A portable model capable of 15 tons an hour was purchased. The department had requested a machine that could mix 90 to 100 1,000-pound batches an hour.

This paragraph leaves the reader with a fuzzy concept of the differences in the equipment because the first sentence describes the output in tons per week, the second in tons per hour, and the third in pounds per hour. Since he probably wouldn't know how many hours per week are involved in the first description, the copyreader wouldn't be able to put all three measures in the same context without talking the problem over with the reporter. But he could at least do this:

> Using the old method, ~~it took~~ the street department took a week to mix 50 tons of blacktop. ~~A portable model capable of 15 tons an hour was purchased.~~ The department ~~had~~ requested a machine that could mix 45 to 50 tons ~~90 to 100 1,000-pound batches~~ an hour, but the city bought a portable model capable of 15 tons an hour.

Misguided Tenses

> He believes that within the next decade computers will become common in the home.

In an interview or personality piece that is not pegged to a particular point in time, expressions like "he believes," "she says," "he argues that," or "she opposes" can be appropriate. If the story is about what a person said at a specific time, however (in a speech or an interview, for example), the past tense is proper and the copyreader should make the appropriate change. Here he might do it this way:

> said he
>
> He believes that within the
>
> next decade computers will become
>
> common in the home.

Archaic Words

> Prof. Barton said Samoan men appear
> to be more contented with their victuals
> than American men.

Except in direct quotations, a speaker's odd language should be translated into modern American English. Few people say "victuals" any more. Nor do they talk of going "motoring," or of driving a "motorcar" or an "auto," or of seeing a "creature" on the road. Outdated language, whether Chaucerian, Shakespearean, or early twentieth-century American, puts a strain on the reader.

The Omnipurpose "Wise"

> He said that, populationwise,
> India faces a grim future.

"Unwise," "likewise," "otherwise," and "clockwise" are legitimate words, but most other *wise* words are of dubious parentage. If "populationwise" should ever make the grade with grammarians, then, theorywise, it would be possible to make every noun in the language do double duty. Practicewise, though, it would be awful.

Wordiness

THE term "wordiness" covers a lot of writing sins: repetition, unnecessary or irrelevant detail, meaningless generalization, and roundabout phrasing. One of the most common of the space wasters is the sentence that spells out the question put to a news source. It can usually be edited out, as it is in these passages:

Questioned about the ultimate aim of the "Commentator," Mr. Bradshaw said that the goal is to reach a paid circulation large enough to make the newspaper self-sustaining.

~~Questioned about the ultimate aim of the "Commentator,"~~ Mr. Bradshaw said ~~that~~ the goal *of the "Commentator"* is to *get enough* ~~reach a~~ paid circulation ~~large enough~~ to *be* ~~make the newspaper~~ self-sustaining.

* * *

Asked his opinion on the Speakers Rule, he replied that his one-word summation is not printable, but he followed with, "I don't like it."

He said ~~Asked~~ his opinion ~~on~~ of the Speakers Rule~~, he replied that his one word summation~~ is ~~not~~ un print-able. ~~but he followed with, "I don't like it."~~

* * *

Asked whether dormitory design is usually considered such a specialized field, he said, "It can be and we have made it such."

He said ~~Asked whether~~ dormitory design ~~is usually~~ has become ~~considered such~~ a specialized field. ~~he said, "It can be and we have made it such."~~

* * *

When asked whether there were any state laws prohibiting integration of state institutions or coed dances between inmates of state institutions, McLane said, "absolutely none."

McLane said state law does not ~~When asked whether there were any state laws~~ prohibit~~ing~~ integration or ~~of state institutions or~~ coed dances ~~between inmates of~~ at state institutions. ~~McLane said, "absolutely none."~~

* * *

When questioned as to his views on book banning, Mr. Goshorn said it is ridiculous.

~~When questioned as to his views on book banning,~~ Mr. Goshorn said ~~it~~ (book banning) is ridiculous.

* * *

Asked if he could foresee any changes being made because of these charges, he answered: "We don't plan to change our policy in any way."

(As to the effect of the) ~~Asked if he could foresee any changes being made because of these~~ charges, he ~~answered:~~ (said:) "We don't plan to change our policy in any way."

* * *

When he was asked to comment about the possibility of former Alabama Gov. George Wallace's coming to the campus to speak, he said, "There is nothing in our rule to keep Gov. Wallace from speaking here."

(He said there is nothing in the rule to keep) ~~When he was asked to comment about the possibility of~~ former Alabama Gov. George Wallace ~~'s coming to~~ (from speaking on) the campus. ~~to speak, he said, "There is nothing in our rule to keep Gov. Wallace from speaking here."~~

* * *

```
    Mr. Humphrey was asked if he is betraying
his liberal principles.  He replied, "Liberalism
is the law of the land."
```

Oh. Next question.

Related to the needless question is the needless comment on, or explanation of, the speaker's subject. If the story reports clearly what the speaker says, it should not have to explain what he is talking about. Yet some do it, in a variety of ways:

```
    To illustrate the unity
between Sen. Metcalf and the
President, he said . . .
```

(Better: "He said . . .")

```
    Speaking on "Punishment
and Rehabilitation," Eshelman
pointed out that punishment
and rehabilitation are different
means to the same end.
```

(Better: "Eshelman said that punishment and rehabilitation are different means to the same end.")

```
    To clarify what he meant by punishment
of the prisoners, Eshelman began with a
description of the fortress-like appearance
of San Quentin.
```

(Better: "Eshelman said San Quentin looks like a fortress.")

Note also in the examples above that "described" would be shorter and more forceful than "began with a description of." The reader doesn't care whether he began with it, ended with it, or stuck it somewhere in the middle. The reporter should select the most important or most interesting elements of a speech, regardless of their position, and rearrange them to his liking.

The copyreader should delete useless sentences like these:

```
    Before getting into the dis-
cussion, he made some opening
remarks to the audience.

    This was the first point
the speaker made in his lecture.
```

And he should improve this one by trimming, as indicated:

> Mr. Bradley made one last comment on the character of the town. "It is an elegant version of Peyton Place," he said.

> Mr. Bradley ~~made one last comment on the character of~~ described the town, ~~"It is~~ as an elegant version of Peyton Place." ~~he said.~~

The irrelevant detail, often in the form of a generality plucked from the air, is another common space waster. This lead, from a feature story about an actress turned housemother, is typical:

> Many of the girls who live in the rooming house at 65 E. 13th Ave. don't know that their housemother is a 40-year veteran of stage, radio and television.

The copyreader should ask himself whether this story is about the housemother or the ignorance of the girls she mothers. If it's about the housemother, which it is, he could edit this way:

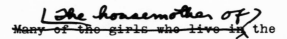

> The housemother of ~~Many of the girls who live in~~ the rooming house at 65 E. 13th Ave. ~~don't know that their housemother~~ is a 40-year veteran of stage, radio and television.

Here's a lead from a story about what goes on behind the scenes before and during a lecture at a huge university:

> A student sitting in a classroom may not realize what minor jobs must be done in preparation for a television lecture.

Indeed, he may not. But if the story is about the preparations, and not about the student sitting in the classroom, it could be edited this way:

> ~~A student sitting in a classroom~~ ~~may not realize what minor~~ many small jobs must be done ~~in preparation~~ to get things ready for a television lecture.

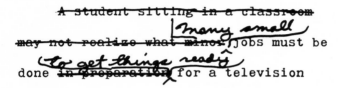

Wordiness may change the writer's meaning. A campus editorial urging changes in the divorce laws said this:

> In the United States, we have progressed to the point where church and state are no longer united, but this progression has not appreciably affected divorce laws.

What the writer meant to say was that, despite the constitutional separation of church and state, divorce laws in the United States are still rooted in religious doctrine. But by taking such a roundabout approach he has implied that church and state were not always separate in this country.

Another example is from a story on a speech by a foreign correspondent who went to Vietnam a hawk and returned a dove:

> Mrs. Halstead said her opinion of the war was no longer that of the administration in Washington, D.C.

The implication is that she remained constant while the administration changed its views. Try this instead: "Mrs. Halstead said she no longer agrees with the administration's war policies."

And finally:

```
     They will complete the tour
in the southeastern portion of the
United States, in the vicinity of
Florida.
```

Like Georgia, or Alabama, or eleven miles off shore?

Most of the time, wordiness doesn't change meaning; it just makes the meaning harder to grasp. Verbiage comes by the paragraph, the sentence, or the phrase. The wordy paragraph often announces itself by declining to come to the point. It opens with a generality that leads to a specific, and winds up with needless duplication of ideas. For example:

```
     Forgey pointed out that there was no

question as to the popularity of the

Liverpool, England, singing group.  After

all, in his own record shop he has sold

over 200 Beatle albums in the last two weeks.
```

Here the number of sales points up the popularity of the group and makes the first sentence superfluous. So the copyreader could do this:

Forgey *said* ~~pointed out that there was no~~

~~question as to the popularity of the~~

~~Liverpool, England, singing group. After~~

~~all, in~~ his ~~own~~ record shop ~~he~~ has sold

more than ~~over~~ 200 Beatle albums in the last two weeks.

Again:

```
     Chapman noted that one of the main

functions of the new center will be to
```

provide a varied program of recreation for the students. Included in the new facility will be 10 bowling lanes, a 19-table billiard room . . .

Try this:

Chapman said ~~noted that one of the main functions of~~ the new center will have ~~be to provide a varied program of recreation for the students. Included in the new facility will be~~ 10 bowling lanes, a 19-table billiard room . . .

And again:

The first person interviewed was LaRue Nelson, a Negro sociology major from New Orleans. He said he is "satisfied" with his existence as a Negro in this community. Nelson claims the only case of discrimination against him was by high school students on a downtown street. He said they called him "nigger" and told him to "go back to the Job Corps."

Try this:

> ~~The first person interviewed was~~
>
> LaRue Nelson, a black ~~Negro~~ sociology major
>
> from New Orleans, said that some ~~He said he is~~
>
> ~~"satisfied" with his existence as a~~
>
> ~~Negro in this community. Nelson~~
>
> ~~claims the only case of discrimination~~
>
> ~~against him was by~~ high school students once,
>
> ~~on a downtown street. He said they~~ called
>
> him "nigger" and told him to "go back
>
> to the Job Corps," but that otherwise he has felt no discrimination in the community.

Sentences, too, can circle warily about a point instead of driving straight at it. It happens when the reporter tries to be fancy and winds up being pompous, like this:

> He pointed out that over the period of time when the government of the mainland has been China's functioning leadership, they have produced many great things.

It means: "He pointed out that, under Communist rule, China has made great technological progress."

And this:

> According to Sen. Mansfield the continuing of a negative United States attitude toward trade with China has "added venom" to the system of U.S.-Chinese relations.

It means: "Sen. Mansfield said that the United States' refusal to trade with China has added 'venom' to U.S.-Chinese relations."

And this:

> China has, according to the senator, asserted its will to support wars of liberation, but it has not taken direct involvement in any such wars.

It means: "The senator said China has supported wars of national liberation, but has not become directly involved in them."

And this:

> Sen. Mansfield said that the military involvements which have occurred on the Chinese boundaries, first Korea and now Vietnam, are due to a lack of communications between China and the United States.

It means: "Sen. Mansfield said the wars in Korea and Vietnam would not have occurred if China and the United States had been on speaking terms."

And this:

> This would help in creating an attitude among the Chinese of improving the trend of relations.

It means: "This would make the Chinese friendlier."

Small wonder Americans have trouble communicating with Chinese.

One way to cut down on verbiage is to watch the verbs. Often one tidy short verb can be substituted for a sloppy long phrase, as in these passages:

> He did not engage in slander of
>
> his opponent or defense of himself.

> He did not ~~engage in~~ slander ~~of~~
>
> his opponent or defend ~~defense of~~ himself.

* * *

> She painted a word picture of Japan
>
> as a land of paradoxes.

> She pictured ~~painted a word picture of~~ Japan
>
> as a land of paradoxes.

* * *

He gave a detailed account of the processes.

described

He ~~gave a detailed account of~~ the processes in detail.

* * *

He said there has been less of an increase in the cost of living in the last three months than in the preceding three.

has increased less

He said ~~there has been less of an increase in~~ the cost of living in the last three months than in the preceding three.

* * *

Views expressed against him were of the general consensus that the only reason he was re-elected was because people are narrow-minded and afraid of change.

His opponents said

~~Views expressed against him were of the general consensus that the only reason~~ he was re-elected ~~was~~ because people are narrow-minded and afraid of change.

* * *

    She cited the fact that at present
    all baking is done in the Royer Commons
    kitchen.

She ~~cited the fact~~ (noted) that ~~at present~~ all baking is done in the Royer Commons kitchen.

Perhaps most frequently, sentences fatten on repetition, redundancy, the passive voice, and the statement of the obvious. Here are some typical examples, with translations:

    Mike's specialty is track, namely
    the 100- and 220-yard dashes.

(Mike is a sprinter.)

* * *

    He busies himself by taking color slides.

(He takes color slides.)

* * *

    Another shortcut is the fact that
    potatoes and carrots come already peeled.

(Potatoes and carrots are peeled before delivery.)

* * *

    The fact that racial prejudice seems
    not to exist in Siebert Hall was the basis
    for remarks made by head resident Miss
    Marita Bricker.

(Siebert Hall is apparently free from racial prejudice, according to Miss Marita Bricker, head resident.)

* * *

Her initial interest began six years ago.

(She became interested six years ago.)

* * *

Anderson does not favor the state sales tax as a means of raising revenue.

(Anderson opposes the sales tax.)

* * *

He got his secondary schooling from Rice University, where he received his B.A.

(He received his B.A. from Rice University.)

* * *

He enjoys watching TV westerns with his wife and four children in their home.

(He enjoys watching TV westerns with his wife and four children.)

* * *

The YWCA will be encouraged in the total of $9,500 to be given to that organization.

(The YWCA will get $9,500.)

* * *

Another interesting and unusual fact about the dormitory is that it will be coeducational.

(The dormitory will be coeducational.)

* * *

One of the main and most frequent sources of information comes from University housemothers.

(Housemothers provide much information.)

* * *

```
    She explained that teachers must have
a thorough knowledge of anatomy and physiology
in order to understand the skeletal
structure and the functions of the
various muscles of the body.
```

(She said teachers must understand the skeletal structure and muscle functions.)

* * *

```
    He announced his belief that 18-year-olds
should be given the right to vote.
```

(He said 18-year-olds should have the right to vote.)

* * *

```
    She then leveled a criticism at the
secrecy surrounding the way in which sororities
extend bids and conduct Rush Week activities.
```

(She criticized the secrecy that surrounds Rush Week.)

* * *

```
    He holds a B.A. in the field of political
science.
```

(He holds a B.A. in political science.)

The fat sentence also feeds on the elongated phrase. "At the present time" usually means "now," "he went on to add" usually means "he added," and "it is possible for a man to" usually means "a man can."

Every word should count.

Style, Conventions, And Spelling

ALL periodicals have idiosyncrasies called "style." These are the rules that govern capitalization, abbreviations, the use of names and numbers, typographical design, and other matters of choice, taste, whim, and fancy.

The rules are usually set forth in a "style book," a publication that can be anything from a few pages of simple guidelines to a hundred or more pages of detailed regulations. Regardless of its length, the copyreader should become thoroughly familiar with it, and keep it near him.

Adherence to style is important not because one style is "correct" but because consistency brings order to the newspaper. While many editors would agree with Emerson's complaint about "foolish consistency," few would find anything foolish in the consistent treatment of titles, street names, dates, cut-lines, and such.

The general impression that a paper gives its readers depends to a considerable extent on grammar, spelling, and consistent style. Furthermore, an adherence to rules of grammar, spelling, and style breeds a sense of discipline in both the reporter and the copyreader. The newsman who is careful about these matters is unlikely to be careless with fact.

Style books cover such points as:

(1) Capitalization. When is it east and when is it East? Is it Council or council, Communist or communist?

(2) Abbreviations. Is it Main Street or Main St., Nebraska or Neb., ROTC or R.O.T.C.?

(3) Punctuation. Is it James Brown Jr. or James Brown, Jr.? William Green of Tulsa or William Green, of Tulsa?

(4) Numbers. Is it nine or 9, ten or 10, 21 million or 21,000,000?

(5) Titles. Is it the secretary of state or the Secretary of State? The President or the president? Dist. Atty. Henry Black or District Attorney Henry Black? Rev. Gray or the Rev. Mr. Gray? Mr. White or Dr. White or Prof. White or Plain Old White?

(6) Spelling. Is it judgment or judgement, likeable or likable, kidnaping or kidnapping, transatlantic or trans-Atlantic, cigaret or cigarette, employe or employee?

(7) Headlines. Is it Storm Heads Out to Sea, or Storm heads out to sea, or STORM HEADS OUT TO SEA?

(8) Typography. Are cutlines and by-lines and credit lines and copyright lines and datelines set this way or that way? What's done with sports summaries, market reports, weather reports, pollen counts, and such?

In addition, most style books go into some detail on local matters, such as the usage of place names and names of governmental agencies, the capitalization of academic departments, the designation of a student's class and major or of an alumnus' class, and the titles of local offices and officials.

Until he knows its contents, front to back, the copyreader should refer to his style book often.

Conventions

The conventions of news writing are allied to style, and vary from region to region and from paper to paper. The copyreader must know what conventions are observed by his office, just as he must know how to use his style book.

On most newspapers you will:

(1) Do more paragraphing than you do in themes, letters, and essays. This is a typographical rather than a grammatical matter. Indentations for paragraphs create white space that relieves the monotony of the long, narrow newspaper column. Usually, there is a paragraph break after each two or three sentences, or after 30 to 50 words.

(2) Put a direct quotation in a separate paragraph. If the reporter hasn't done it, the copyreader handles it like this:

```
        Councilman Robinson accused the mayor
of not knowing his own mind.  "Last month he
opposed all the things he supported today,"
Robinson said.  The mayor declined to comment.
```

(3) Use the first name and middle initial in the first reference to a person. (This convention is ignored by many newspapers in the West, where nicknames are common in the news and editorial columns.)

(4) Use the last name, not the first, in subsequent references to adults and young adults. Style on the use or omission of "Mr." in the second

reference varies, but it is customary to use "Mrs." or "Miss"—never the last name alone—in a second reference to a woman or teen-age girl. In recent years, some newspapers, particularly in the student press, have adopted the last-name-only style for women as well as men, but the complimentary title for women remains the rule on papers of general circulation.

(5) Drop the first name, if it sounds better, in a first reference to a person of prominence, or to one whose name appears frequently, as in: President Nixon, President Pusey (if your paper is the Harvard *Crimson*), Gov. Shapiro (if your paper is in Illinois), Mayor Rizzo (if your paper is in Philadelphia), or Archbishop McIntyre (if your paper is in the Los Angeles area).

(6) Avoid the first-person pronoun. You will change this passage: "He said we must stand firm in our resolve, regardless of world opinion." You will make it read something like this: "He said the United States must stand firm in its resolve, regardless of world opinion."

(7) Use the name and then the office, rather than the office and then the name, in lists of officers, like this: "Other new officers are William Brooks, first vice president; Harry Rivers, second vice president; James Lake, secretary; and Mrs. James L. Pond, treasurer."

(8) Make it "Poole said" rather than "said Poole."

When wire service copy and staff-written material are combined in the same story, it is customary to indicate where one ends and the other begins. Sometimes it is done parenthetically:

```
     Mayor Daley said he had rejected the NBC
proposal, but still had not heard from ABC.
     (According to the Associated Press, an
ABC spokesman in New York said that network
had not received the mayor's request for free
time.)
     CBS announced yesterday that it had re-
jected Daley's proposal.
```

Sometimes the parentheses are dropped:

```
     Mayor Daley said he had rejected the NBC
proposal, but still had not heard from ABC.
     However, the Associated Press quoted an
ABC official in New York as saying that network
had not received the mayor's request for free
time.
     CBS announced yesterday that it had re-
jected Daley's proposal.
```

If a paper uses AP or UPI or Reuter for the coverage of a local story, it drops the dateline but customarily credits the wire service in a by-line or agate line over the story:

```
By the Associated Press
United Press International
AP
By UPI
```

Newcomers are often surprised to learn that the newspaper is free to revamp and cut wire service copy, just as it would change its own. The beginning copyreader should understand that wire services, too, can write inaccurately, verbosely, foolishly, and ungrammatically. This wire service lead should not have made it past the desk:

```
Turkey has apparently won a smashing
political victory in the Cyprus crisis that
nearly plunged the eastern Mediterranean
into war for a few hours.
```

Here the wire service has created a potential companion to the Hundred Years War and the Thirty Years War: The Few Hours War. The copyreader should have done this:

```
Turkey has apparently won a smashing
political victory in the Cyprus crisis that
for a few hours threatened to plunge
~~nearly plunged~~ the eastern Mediterranean
into war ~~for a few hours~~.
```

This paragraph, from a story on a subject that almost always causes trauma, shouldn't have made it, either:

```
Only last Friday the Berrien County
Board of Supervisors reaffirmed a decision
to place the county on Central Daylight
Time, which meant clocks wouldn't be ad-
```

> vanced at all from their then-current Eastern
> Standard Time. This is an hour later than
> the rest of Lower Michigan, which went
> on Eastern Daylight.

Seems clear. Trouble is, Central Daylight and Eastern Standard are an hour earlier than Eastern Daylight. Not later.

There is one convention that is not universally observed, but should be: wire copy should be read with as much skepticism as local copy.

Spelling

If you think you're a good speller, have a friend read this list of words while you write them down:

accommodate	ingenious	battalion
consensus	restaurateur	hypocrisy
harass	Philippines	privilege
strait jacket	embarrass	supersede
Caribbean	fictitious	statistician
impostor	permissible	mischievous
missile	subpoena	indispensable
resuscitator	pastime	inoculate
irresistible	lethargic	connoisseur
cemetery	analyst	dietitian

Now check for accuracy.

If you missed 15, or half, you're about average for a college sophomore or junior. But if you missed more than five and want to be a copyreader, you have some work to do.

The good speller has a double advantage over the mediocre or poor one. He misspells fewer words to begin with, of course, but he is also more likely to know when it's advisable to look a word up. The misspelling looks all right to the poor speller. But it looks wrong to the good speller; even if he isn't sure of the right way, he is suspicious.

The person with a spelling problem can help himself by learning the kinds of words that are most likely to give him trouble. Among the most troublesome types are these:

(1) Words that sound alike: council, counsel; stationery, stationary; principle, principal; missile, missal
(2) Multisyllabic words with double consonants: accommodate, embarrass
(3) Multisyllabic words with single consonants: inoculate, peritonitis
(4) Nouns ending with a "shin" sound: dietitian, statistician

(5) Adjectives ending with a "shus" sound: fictitious, pernicious
(6) Adjectives ending in "ible" or "able": irresistible, indispensable
(7) Words in which the accent seems misplaced: Caribbean, Philippines, harass, battalion
(8) Words ending with an "erry" sound: cemetery, momentary
(9) Words with an "ess" sound: consensus, concession, supersede
(10) Foreign and scientific words: connoisseur, anschluss, pancreaticoduodenostomy.

The best advice: when in doubt, look it up. And do a lot of doubting.

Cutting For Space

In the utopian land of the inverted pyramid, the editor who must cut copy to fit a hole can start with the last paragraph and work his way toward the lead, hacking away mindlessly until he has a story of just the right length. A real copy desk is not utopia, however, and few editors still teach that the inverted pyramid is the ideal structure for most news stories. The material of least interest or importance is not necessarily at the end. When a story must be shortened, changes must be made selectively.

Whether he is making deletions at the copy desk or on the composing room floor, the editor must be sensitive to the language and to the overall meaning of the story. He should cut and suture without leaving either deformity or scar. The story should remain well porportioned and have all its essential parts; there should be no evidence of surgery. Ideally, the story should be left in such good condition that even the writer isn't sure what has been removed.

Cutting is mostly a matter of logic. Above all, it should be orderly. The copyreader should begin by editing routinely, without thought of space. That usually shortens the story somewhat.

Then he can cut for space. The first step is just reediting. The copyreader should try to tighten the story without changing content. He should look for wordiness, repetition, weak modifiers, and needless detail, and he should see whether he can save words by recasting sentences without changing their meaning.

Next he must deal with changes in content. He should begin by looking for material that is not vital to the reader's understanding of the story. Typically, this is stuff that expands on a basic point: a direct quotation that adds color to a paraphrase, for example, or in a golf story a list of the holes on which the victor shot his birdies and bogies.

Not until he reaches this point should the copyreader make any significant change in content. Now he must do so, but the paring should be reasoned and logical. The least important of what remains should go out first. If several items seem to be equally important, the least interesting should go. There is no rule of thumb for determining importance. One factor which must be considered, however, is whether the deletion of a fact would leave an unanswered question. If it would, that fact is important.

To illustrate the trimming process, let's look at three stories and the steps the copyreader might go through in cutting them. One must be cut by about a third, another by half, and the last by two thirds.

First, from the *San Francisco Chronicle*, a local story, 287 words long, that we'll assume has to be cut to about 200 words to fill a 1-column hole eight inches deep:

San Francisco Sheriff Matthew Carberry yesterday denied that the county jail's medical care program is suffering from anything more serious than a somewhat anemic budget.

He said a long list of charges made by Dr. Pat Stalteri, the jail's parttime physician, were "grossly exaggerated and often ridiculous."

Stalteri told the mayor's Advisory Committee on Adult Detention Wednesday that the jail currently is encountering drug shortages, threats of disease, overcrowding and unbalanced prisoner diets.

Carberry said "it's a case of cost versus need, and the public pays the bills. We live with the budget problem continually."

"It's still a very good county jail system," he said.

Carberry said the reason Stalteri had been informed of only one of four inmate deaths this year probably was that three of the four men had died at San Francisco Hospital. He said each of the three, all of whom died of liver ailments connected with alcoholism, had been taken to the hospital the day they were received at the jail.

He said the case of the fourth man, who was taken to the hospital for treatment but who was listed as dead on arrival, is still being investigated by the coroner.

Carberry quoted the coroner as saying the amount of chloral hydrate the man had received from a deputy sheriff "had nothing to do with the man's death."

The sheriff also denied that the jail has had any problem getting milk for patients with ulcer conditions.

He said the jail is "well and adequately supplied with drugs at the present time, and we look forward to no problems."

```
        He termed "exaggerated" Stalteri's claim
    that 50 per cent of the 700 prisoners are
    suffering from blanket rashes because there are
    no sheets at the jail.
```

Now let's go through the trimming process, step by step.

STEP 1

Tighten the copy, looking for wordiness, repetition, unnecessary detail.

(1) Delete "a long list of."

(2) Change "currently is encountering" to "faces."

(3) Change "prisoner diets" to "diets."

(4) Delete the quotation, "It's still a very good county jail system."

(5) Change "each of the three, all of whom died of" to "these three had," and change "had been" to "and were."

(6) Change "who was taken to the hospital for treatment but who was listed as dead on arrival" to "who was listed as dead on arrival at the hospital."

(7) Delete "by the coroner."

(8) Change "the amount of chloral hydrate the man had received from a deputy sheriff 'had nothing to do with the man's death' " to "the man's death was not related to the amount of sedation he had received from a deputy sheriff."

(9) Change "ulcer conditions" to "ulcers."

(10) Change "He said the jail is 'well and adequately supplied with drugs at the present time, and we look forward to no problems' " to "He said the jail has enough drugs and expects no problems."

(11) Change "there are no sheets at the jail" to "the jail has no sheets."

The net saving in Step 1 is 49 words, and the story now reads like this:

```
        San Francisco Sheriff Matthew Carberry
    yesterday denied that the county jail's medical
    care program is suffering from anything more
    serious than a somewhat anemic budget.
        He said ~~a long list of~~ charges made by
```

Dr. Pat Stalteri, the jail's parttime physician, were "grossly exaggerated and often ridiculous."

Stalteri told the mayor's Advisory Committee on Adult Detention Wednesday that the jail ~~currently is encountering~~ faces drug shortages, threats of disease, overcrowding and unbalanced ~~prisoner~~ diets.

Carberry said "it's a case of cost versus need, and the public pays the bills. We live with the budget problem continually."

~~"It's still a very good county jail system," he said.~~

Carberry said the reason Stalteri had been informed of only one of four inmate deaths this year probably was that three of the four men had died at San Francisco Hospital. He said ~~each of the~~ these three, had ~~all of whom died of~~ liver ailments connected with alcoholism, ~~had been~~ and were taken to the hospital the day they were received at the jail.

He said the case of the fourth man, who was ~~taken to the hospital for treatment but who was~~

listed as dead on arrival *at the hospital* is still being

investigated ~~by the coroner~~.

Carberry quoted the coroner as saying the
man's death was not related to the amount of sedation
~~amount of chloral hydrate the man had received~~
he had received
from a deputy sheriff ~~"had nothing to do with~~

~~the man's death."~~

The sheriff also denied that the jail has

had any problem getting milk for patients

with ulcers ~~conditions.~~

He said the jail *has enough drugs and expects* ~~is "well and adequately~~

~~supplied with drugs at the present time, and~~

~~we look forward to~~ no problems. ~~"~~

He termed "exaggerated" Stalteri's claim

that 50 per cent of the 700 prisoners are

suffering from blanket rashes because ~~there are~~

~~no sheets at~~ the jail *has no sheets*

#

STEP 2

Continue to tighten the story, looking for expendable words and phrases, and for details that are not vital to meaning. Delete peripheral information.

(1) Change "told the mayor's Advisory Committee on Adult Detention" to "said."

(2) Change "who was listed as dead on arrival" to "who was dead on arrival."

(3) Delete the paragraph in which the sheriff quotes the coroner. (The investigation has not been completed, the opinion is secondhand, and the significance of the comment is not explained.)

(4) Delete "and expects no problems."

The net saving in Step 2 is 37 words, and the story now looks like this:

San Francisco Sheriff Matthew Carberry yesterday denied that the county jail's medical care program is suffering from anything more serious than a somewhat anemic budget.

He said ~~a long list of~~ charges made by Dr. Pat Stalteri, the jail's parttime physician, were "grossly exaggerated and often ridiculous."

Stalteri said ~~told the mayor's Advisory Committee on Adult Detention~~ Wednesday that the jail faces ~~currently is encountering~~ drug shortages, threats of disease, overcrowding and unbalanced ~~prisoner~~ diets.

Carberry said "it's a case of cost versus need, and the public pays the bills. We live with the budget problem continually."

~~"It's still a very good county jail system," he said.~~

Carberry said the reason Stalteri had been informed of only one of four inmate deaths this year probably was that three of the four men had died at San Francisco Hospital. He said these ~~each of the~~ three, had ~~all of whom died of~~

liver ailments connected with alcoholism, ~~had~~ [and were] ~~been~~ taken to the hospital the day they were received at the jail.

He said the case of the fourth man, who was ~~taken to the hospital for treatment but who was listed as~~ dead on arrival [at the hospital,] is still being investigated ~~by the coroner.~~

~~Carberry quoted the coroner as saying the~~ [man's death was not related to the amount of sedation] ~~amount of chloral hydrate the man had received~~ [he had received] ~~from a deputy sheriff "had nothing to do with the man's death."~~

The sheriff also denied that the jail has had any problem getting milk for patients with ulcer~~s conditions.~~

He said the jail [has enough drugs] ~~and expects~~ ~~is "well and adequately supplied with drugs at the present time, and we look forward to no problems."~~

He termed "exaggerated" Stalteri's claim that 50 per cent of the 700 prisoners are suffering from blanket rashes because ~~there are no sheets at~~ the jail [has no sheets.]

Note that the changes made in the first step, while substantially reduc-
g the length, leave the story virtually intact as far as content is con-

cerned. The only substantive deletion is the sheriff's remark, "It's still a very good county jail system." But, except for Dr. Stalteri's attack on the medical care program, no one has said it isn't. Hence the comment seems irrelevant.

Step 2 eliminates a fact that could be important: the sheriff's reference to the coroner's comment about the cause of a death. But the story does not show the significance of the remark. If Dr. Stalteri said something that conflicted with the coroner's view, the story does not say so, and therefore the reference seems to be of minor importance.

Mine is not the only way to edit this story, of course. Some newsmen might argue that the coroner's statement is imore important than the paragraph about the blanket rashes, or the sheriff's remark about cost versus need, or his denial that the jail has trouble getting milk. And they might make a sound case. The important point to remember is that while there may be differences in judgment the editing is based on reasoning, not impulse.

Now let's look at an Associated Press story, as it appeared in the *Los Angeles Times*, and assume that it must be cut from about 250 words to about 125 in order to fit a hole four inches deep.

WASHINGTON (AP) — A prestigious American scientific organization Friday urged a U.N.-sponsored field study — in the heart of the Vietnam war zone — to determine whether there might be long-term adverse effects from military use of defoliant chemicals.

It said the Defense Department may be overconfident that no such hazard exists.

The American Association for the Advancement of Science urged also that scientists making any such study be protected "by the contending forces in the area."

The association's board — in a statement published in Science, the organization's official journal — also urged that American forces temporarily suspend use of arsenical herbicides rated as potentially the most hazardous from a long-term environmental standpoint of all herbicides used militarily.

The board said that, on the basis of its own study of available information, it does "not share the confidence expressed by the Department of Defense that seriously adverse consequences will not occur as a result of the use of herbicide chemicals in Vietnam, insofar as arsenical compounds are concerned."

The 12-member board, headed by Dr. Don K. Price of Harvard University, retiring president of the AAAS, declared:

"If rehabilitation of lands adversely affected by these agents is required, ecological environmental studies initiated now will be of substantial value in defining the required programs. If defoliation has produced or can produce beneficial influences on the food-producing capacity of the affected regions, these possibilities should be evaluated fully so that they can be most effectively exploited for the benefit of the Vietnamese people."

Now let's edit.

Step 1

Tighten the copy. Look for wordiness, repetition, and unnecessary detail.

(1) Change "A prestigious American scientific organization" to "The American Association for the Advancement of Science."

(2) Change "in the heart of the Vietnam war zone" to "in Vietnam."

(3) Delete "The American Association for the Advancement of Science," since this name now appears in the lead.

(4) Change "any such" to "the" and "forces in the area" to "armies."

(5) Delete "in a statement published in *Science*, the organization's official journal."

(6) Change "the most hazardous from a long-term environmental standpoint of all herbicides used militarily" to "the most hazardous of the defoliants."

(7) Delete "of available information."

The net saving in Step 1 is 36 words, and the story now reads like this:

WASHINGTON (AP) — ~~A prestigious American scientific organization~~ The American Association for the Advancement of Science Friday urged a U.N.-sponsored field study ~~in the heart of the Vietnam war zone~~ in Vietnam to determine whether there might be long-term adverse effects from military use of defoliant chemicals.

It said the Defense Department may be overconfident that no such hazard exists, and proposed

~~The American Association for the Advancement of Science urged also~~ that scientists making ~~any such~~ the study be protected "by the contending ~~forces in the area."~~ armies."

The association's board ~~— in a statement published in Science, the organization's official journal —~~ also urged that American forces temporarily suspend use of arsenical herbicides, rated as potentially the most hazardous ~~from a long-term environmental standpoint of all herbicides used militarily.~~ of the defoliants.

The board said that, on the basis of its own study, ~~of available information,~~ it does "not share the confidence expressed by the Department of Defense that seriously adverse consequences will not occur as a result of the use of herbicide chemicals in Vietnam, insofar as arsenical compounds are concerned."

The 12-member board, headed by Dr. Don K. Price of Harvard University, retiring president of the AAAS, declared:

"If rehabilitation of lands adversely

affected by these agents is required, ecological environmental studies initiated now will be of substantial value in defining the required programs. If defoliation has produced or can produce beneficial influences on the food-producing capacity of the affected regions, these possibilities should be evaluated fully so that they can be most effectively exploited for the benefit of the Vietnamese people."

#

STEP 2

Begin deleting information. Start with the least important. Look for material that enlarges on points that are made elsewhere, and for details that are not vital to understanding the story.

(1) Delete the paragraph beginning "The board said that, on the basis of its own study. . . ."

(2) Delete "headed by Dr. Don K. Price of Harvard University, retiring president of the AAAS."

The net saving in Step 2 is 60 words, and the story now looks like this:

WASHINGTON (AP) — ~~A prestigious American scientific organization~~ The American Association for the Advancement of Science Friday urged a U.N.-sponsored field study ~~— in the heart of the Vietnam war zone —~~ in Vietnam to determine whether there might be long-term adverse effects from military use of defoliant chemicals.

It said the Defense Department may be overconfident that no such hazard exists~~,~~ and proposed

The American Association for the Advancement of Science urged also that scientists making any such study be protected "by the contending forces in the area."

The association's board, in a statement published in Science, the organization's official journal also urged that American forces temporarily suspend use of arsenical herbicides, rated as potentially the most hazardous from a long-term environmental standpoint of all herbicides used militarily.

The board said that, on the basis of its own study, of available information, it does "not share the confidence expressed by the Department of Defense that seriously adverse consequences will not occur as a result of the use of herbicide chemicals in Vietnam, insofar as arsenical compounds are concerned."

The 12-member board, headed by Dr. Don K. Price of Harvard University, retiring president of the AAAS, declared:

"If rehabilitation of lands adversely

affected by these agents is required, ecological environmental studies initiated now will be of substantial value in defining the required programs. If defoliation has produced or can produce beneficial influences on the food-producing capacity of the affected regions, these possibilities should be evaluated fully so that they can be most effectively exploited for the benefit of the Vietnamese people."

STEP 3

Continue deleting, again in inverse order of the importance of the material.

(1) Delete the entire paragraph beginning "The association's board also urged that American forces temporarily suspend. . . ." (It is an important and interesting suggestion, but the proposal for the study is complete and understandable without it.)

(2) Delete "12-member."

The net saving in Step 3 is 25 words, and the story ends up looking like this:

WASHINGTON (AP) — ~~A prestigious American scientific organization~~ *The American Association for the Advancement of Science* Friday urged a U.N.-sponsored field study ~~— in the heart of the Vietnam war zone —~~ *in Vietnam* to determine whether there might be long-term adverse effects from military use of defoliant chemicals.

It said the Defense Department may be overconfident that no such hazard exists *and proposed*

~~The American Association for the Advancement of Science urged also~~ that scientists making ~~any such~~ *the* study be protected "by the contending ~~forces in the area."~~ *armies*

The association's board ~~— in a statement published in Science, the organization's official journal —~~ also urged that American forces temporarily suspend use of arsenical herbicides, rated as potentially the most hazardous ~~from a long term environmental standpoint of all herbicides used militarily.~~ *of the defoliants*

The board said that, on the basis of its own study ~~of available information,~~ it does "not share the confidence expressed by the Department of Defense that seriously adverse consequences will not occur as a result of the use of herbicide chemicals in Vietnam, insofar as arsenical compounds are concerned."

The ~~12-member~~ board ~~headed by Dr. Don K. Price of Harvard University, retiring president of the AAAS,~~ declared:

"If rehabilitation of lands adversely

affected by these agents is required, ecological environmental studies initiated now will be of substantial value in defining the required programs. If defoliation has produced or can produce beneficial influences on the food-producing capacity of the affected regions, these possibilities should be evaluated fully so that they can be most effectively exploited for the benefit of the Vietnamese people."

#

In three steps, the story has been reduced from 248 words to 127—close enough to the 125-word maximum so that it should fit the hole it's designed for. If it's still a line or two long, the second sentence can be chopped off at "exists," and the story will still be complete and clear, as far as it goes.

Despite the extensive deletions, the revised version lacks only four facts that were in the original. One is the board's proposal that American forces suspend the use of arsenical herbicides. This is important, but as noted it is not essential to the central point. The others are relatively minor: that the study proposal was made in *Science*, that the board has twelve members, and that its chairman is Dr. Price.

To an audience of scholars the reference to *Science* might be important, and a newspaper in Boston would probably want to retain the name of Dr. Price. Special considerations like these always influence the editing. Once again, the guiding principle is that the copyreader must have a good reason for what he does.

Now let's look at the hardest problem: reducing a 240-word Reuter story to 80 words to fit it into a two-inch hole in the *Chicago Tribune*.

WASHINGTON (Reuter) — The President's top inflation-fighters today issued a stern warning that the United States is still on a "dangerous road" of excessive wage and price increases.

The cabinet committee on price stability issued a statement to make clear that a recently passed anti-inflation tax increase has to be accompanied by restraint in the private economy, spokesmen said.

The committee was set up by the President in February to study the sources of inflation. It is headed by Arthur Okun, chief presidential economic adviser, and includes the budget director and the secretaries of labor, commerce, and the Treasury.

The group, in its first general statement on the economy, called on business and labor to "exercise utmost restraint in their wage and price decisions."

The statement said prices are still rising by 4 per cent a year, while wages are rising 6 to 7 per cent a year.

"The public interest is clearly violated by any price increases that widen profit margins and any wage settlements that extend the recent disturbing pattern," the committee said.

Asked if a wage settlement of more than 6 per cent in current steel industry negotiations — where failure could bring a nationwide strike Aug. 1 — would violate the public interest, a committee spokesman said it was not commenting specifically on steel.

But the committee wanted wage and price decisions "to be less rather than more, this shoe fits everybody who makes wage and price decisions," he said.

Now let's edit.

STEP 1

Because of the great reduction needed, abandon normal procedure and cut the copy radically by deleting whole paragraphs, if possible. Delete material on organizational structure and history. Then tighten the copy, looking for wordiness, repetition, and unnecessary detail.

(1) Delete paragraph 3.

(2) Change "The President's top inflation-fighters" to "A presidential committee that is studying the sources of inflation."

(3) Change "issued a stern warning" to "warned," placed before "today."

(4) Change "The cabinet committee on price stability" to "It."

(5) In paragraph 4, delete the phrase "in its first general statement on the economy."

(6) Change "The statement" to "It," delete "by," change "while wages are rising" to "and wages," and delete "a year."

(7) Delete the entire last paragraph. (It is repetitious.)

The net saving in Step 1 is 83 words, and the story looks like this:

A presidential committee that is
WASHINGTON (Reuter) — ~~The President's top~~
studying the sources of inflation warned today
~~inflation-fighters today issued a stern warning~~

that the United States is still on a "dangerous road" of excessive wage and price increases.

It
The cabinet committee on price stability issued a statement to make clear that a recently passed anti-inflation tax increase has to be accompanied by restraint in the private economy, spokesmen said.

The committee was set up by the President in February to study the sources of inflation. It is headed by Arthur Okun, chief presidential economic adviser, and includes the budget director and the secretaries of labor, commerce, and the Treasury.

The group, in its first general statement on the economy, called on business and labor to "exercise utmost restraint in their wage and price decisions."

It
The statement said prices are still rising by 4 per cent a year, and while wages are rising 6 to 7 per cent a year.

"The public interest is clearly violated by any price increases that widen profit margins and any wage settlements that extend the recent disturbing pattern," the committee said.

Asked if a wage settlement of more than 6 per cent in current steel industry negotiations — where failure could bring a nationwide strike Aug. 1 — would violate the public interest, a committee spokesman said it was not commenting specifically on steel. #

But the committee wanted wage and price decisions "to be less rather than more, this shoe fits everybody who makes wage and price decisions," he said.

STEP 2

Cut radically again, looking particularly for peripheral details and for general information that may be implicit in actions or comments.

(1) Delete paragraph 2. (The tax increase is incidental to the basic point of the story, while the call for restraint is repeated in the direct quotation in paragraph 4.)

(2) Delete paragraph 4. (The call for restraint is covered by the direct quotation in paragraph 6.)

The net saving in Step 2 is 43 words, and the story now looks like this:

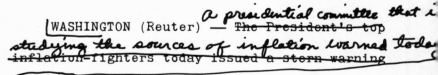

WASHINGTON (Reuter) — a presidential committee that is studying the sources of inflation warned today ~~The President's top inflation-fighters today issued a stern warning~~ that the United States is still on a "dangerous road" of excessive wage and price increases.

The ~~The cabinet committee on price stability~~

issued a statement to make clear that a recently passed anti-inflation tax increase has to be accompanied by restraint in the private economy, spokesmen said.

The committee was set up by the President in February to study the sources of inflation. It is headed by Arthur Okun, chief presidential economic adviser, and includes the budget director and the secretaries of labor, commerce, and the Treasury.

The group, in its first general statement on the economy, called on business and labor to "exercise utmost restraint in their wage and price decisions."

The statement said prices are still rising by 4 per cent a year, while wages are rising 6 to 7 per cent a year.

"The public interest is clearly violated by any price increases that widen profit margins and any wage settlements that extend the recent disturbing pattern," the committee said.

Asked if a wage settlement of more than 6 per cent in current steel industry negotiations —

where failure could bring a nationwide strike Aug. 1 — would violate the public interest, a committee spokesman said it was not commenting specifically on steel.

#

~~But the committee wanted wage and price decisions "to be less rather than more, this shoe fits everybody who makes wage and price decisions," he said.~~

STEP 3

Delete about 30 percent of what remains, looking for material that is least essential to the meaning of the story.

(1) Add this sentence: "It called for restraint by labor and management."

(2) Delete the paragraph beginning "The public interest. . . ."

(3) Edit the "asked if" paragraph to read: "The committee did not refer specifically to the steel industry, where failure of negotiations could bring a nationwide strike Aug. 1."

The net saving in Step 3 is 39 words, and here is the story, now cut to 75 words from its original 240:

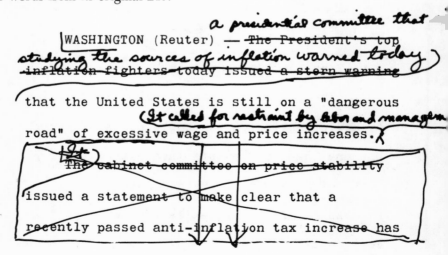

a presidential committee that

WASHINGTON (Reuter) — ~~The President's top~~

studying the sources of inflation warned today

~~inflation fighters today issued a stern warning~~

that the United States is still on a "dangerous

It called for restraint by labor and management

road" of excessive wage and price increases.

It

~~The cabinet committee on price stability issued a statement to make clear that a recently passed anti-inflation tax increase has~~

to be accompanied by restraint in the private economy, spokesmen said.

The committee was set up by the President in February to study the sources of inflation. It is headed by Arthur Okun, chief presidential economic adviser, and includes the budget director and the secretaries of labor, commerce, and the Treasury.

The group, ~~in its first general statement on the economy,~~ called on business and labor to "exercise utmost restraint in their wage and price decisions."

~~The statement~~ [It] said prices are still rising ~~by~~ 4 per cent a year, ~~while~~ [and] wages ~~are rising~~ 6 to 7 per cent ~~a year~~.

"The public interest is clearly violated by any price increases that widen profit margins and any wage settlements that extend the recent disturbing pattern," the committee said.

~~Asked if a wage settlement of more than 6 per cent in current steel industry negotiations where failure~~ [The committee did not refer specifically to the steel industry, where failure of negotiations] could bring a nationwide strike

Aug. 1, would violate the public interest, a committee spokesman said it was not commenting specifically on steel.

But the committee wanted wage and price decisions "to be less rather than more, this shoe fits everybody who makes wage and price decisions," he said.

The hatchet work on this one has been pretty brutal, but note that the essential fact remains: a presidential committee has urged restraint in the interest of curbing inflation.

Editorializing And Editorials

A WRITER cannot be completely objective. If only in the selection and rejection of material, he is bound to be influenced by his convictions, opinions, and prejudices.

The competent reporter is aware of that and makes a conscious effort to keep his feelings out of his work. The copyreader can help him by spotting misplaced emphases, irrelevancies, holes in the story, and expressions of opinion.

In a story about a Marine Corps recruiter in a college town, editorializing looked like this:

```
     To many members of the armed forces,
recruiting duty is known as choice duty.  Any
who are aware of the aspects of it as described
in this article would definitely prefer
being in a line company, rather than re-
porting the consequences of what happens in
a line company to those it hits hardest.
```

The story that began this way turned out to be an interesting and moving account of a recruiter's role in notifying the family and helping with funeral arrangements when a Marine from his area was killed in action. The reporter should have gone right at the story, letting the facts speak for themselves. Unless he is part of the story, the reporter should stay out of it. If he doesn't, the copyreader should muscle him away.

The problem is different in editorials, reviews, and columns of opinion, where judgments are essential. But the editorial or review or column should still be objective in the sense that its conclusions are based on fact and reflect the writer's argument rather than his personality.

The use of the first-person singular can weaken criticism by making the critic seem unsure of himself. "I felt the plot was weak" is an apologetic statement that encourages disagreement. "The plot was weak" is stronger; it defies the reader to disagree. Here are two other critical comments that need strengthening:

```
      To me, this play has qualities of
reality that draw me into the conflicts
of the characters.

      I was unable to figure out what part
the title played in the film.
```

Neither passage requires the first person. Each would be stronger without it. Like this:

```
      The realism involves the audience
in the conflicts of the characters.

      The significance of the title is
not clear.
```

The copyreader may never handle an editorial or a review, for editorial writers and critics are often privileged characters, exempt from the rules that govern mere mortals. If he does, though, he should watch for all the problems he looks for in news copy, plus a few others that are particularly likely to be found in opinion pieces.

Lack of logic, for example. An editorial urging a city to undertake a $25,000 park development project said the job would help the city economically because it would cause construction workers to move to town with their families. A brief consideration of the project's cost would show that to be a nonsensical argument. Any reasonable editorial writer would appreciate the suggestion that it be deleted.

Documentation is another thing to watch. Because of the writer's interest in expressing an opinion, the editorial or critical review may be short on facts. But an opinion is only as good as the facts on which it is based. An editorial that calls for an increase in the number of policemen, for example, should note the size of the force and offer some evidence that it isn't big enough.

Completeness is another problem. An editorial in a college newspaper said federal firearms control legislation would "erode the constitutional right to bear arms and encourage further government distrust of citizens who have no cause to be distrusted." Perhaps so, but the argument is incomplete unless it demonstrates that a right will be eroded, and explains how governmental distrust will be increased.

Another editorial said eight African students, out of twelve interviewed, felt they had been treated badly in America. But it said nothing about the feelings of the other four. Still another said that the university needed a program to attract bright high school students. But the editorial was unconvincing because it didn't explain what good such a program would do.

Vagueness afflicts many editorials. A commentary urging looser divorce laws and tighter marriage laws didn't mean much because it failed to note what requirements needed loosening or tightening.

Absolutes, superlatives, and forceful statements of questionable validity can weaken an argument. This editorial statement might reasonably be challenged: "The School of Pharmacy stands unequalled by any other school on campus in the personal interest that staff members take in students." The same point could be made more effectively with a bit of qualification, like this: "Many students in the School of Pharmacy believe their school is unequalled . . ." or "The School of Pharmacy may be unequalled. . . ." Qualified comments have built-in protection.

The copyreader should also watch out for the broad, unsubstantiated generality. An editorial on rules governing residence off campus said flatly: "Parents favor the idea of having their children live in dormitories." If the reader knows of one parent who doesn't care, or one parent who prefers an off-campus arrangement, he may justifiably question the credibility of the entire editorial. The copyreader might suggest this change: "Many parents favor. . . ." Or, if the statement is based on a survey, he could suggest something like this: "According to a survey by Dean Inloc O. Parentis, most parents. . . ."

Failure to recognize opposing arguments can leave a big hole in an editorial. A demand for the cessation of bombing in North Vietnam, for example, should either concede or counter the contention that the bombing is essential to the safety of American troops in the South. If it does not, the reader may reasonably assume that the writer's argument is based on half-baked thinking. The copyreader should look for such omissions.

Critical reviews may offer subjective judgment as fact. The reviewer has a right to say that the plot of a play is "weak and unrealistic," but the reader has a right to know what's weak about it, and to have an illustration of its lack of realism. A review that praises a writer for an "effective use of metaphors and similes" owes the reader an example of an imaginative metaphor or a vivid simile.

Even if his role in handling a review is that of comma-chaser rather than honest-to-gosh editor, the copyreader should watch for that almost inevitable grammatical slip, the switch in tense. Wrote one reviewer: "There is no dead space in this play. The dialogue was excellent."

Somebody should have done something.

Libel And Fairness

Libel is the publication of false information that hurts someone's reputation.

It may be a reflection on his character: a statement that he is dishonest, or untruthful, or cowardly.

It may be a report that he has done something that is frowned upon by the community: that he uses drugs, or drinks heavily, or is a nudist, or has deserted his wife, or gambles.

It may be a reflection on his professional competence, or his skill at a trade or business, or the quality of the goods or services he sells: a statement that a surgeon is a butcher, or that a teacher is uneducated, or that a builder can't hammer a nail straight, or that a retailer sells sleazy merchandise.

It may be a statement that he has a socially unacceptable disease, such as a venereal infection or alcoholism or a mental disorder.

By the classic legal definition, libel is anything that exposes a person to "hatred, contempt, or ridicule," or damages him in his business or profession, or has a tendency to deter others from associating with him.

Whatever an individual does or says can affect his reputation and the reputations of others, and since newspapers are in business primarily to publish reports of what people do and say they are always in danger of being sued for libel. The copyreader must watch for the warning signals.

If he handles art—photos, cartoons—he must remember that the term "publication" is not limited to the printed word. It means, in essence, anything that constitutes a record. A cartoon can be libelous. So can a picture, particularly if it is retouched (although the chief danger in pictures lies in inaccurate cutlines). Historically, it was "publication" that distinguished libel from the less serious offense of slander, or spoken defamation, but because of their potential for causing damage—and doubtless, too, because of the general practice of taping or recording transcripts—defamatory words spoken on radio and television are generally considered to be libel, not slander. Indeed, courts have held that even conduct can be libelous. A private detective, for example, might check on a person's activities in such an obtrusive way as to injure his reputation, and thus be guilty of libel by conduct.

Most publications spend little time actually fighting libel suits, but the threat is always there. Hardly an issue of the weekly trade magazine *Editor & Publisher* does not have a story of a libel action started or dismissed or tried or concluded or continued on appeal. When the threat materializes, it can wreak economic havoc. A city commissioner and the mayor of Montgomery, Alabama, won jury verdicts of $500,000 each in libel suits against *The New York Times*. Wallace Butts, former football coach and athletic director at the University of Georgia, won a $3,060,000 verdict from the Curtis Publishing Company because of a libelous magazine article. The decision against the *Times* was reversed by the United States Supreme Court and the verdict against Curtis was reduced by the trial judge to $460,000, but the cases illustrate the potential danger. Even if the publisher ultimately wins, he may spend many thousands of dollars on legal costs.

The extent to which student publications may be liable for damages, particularly in tax-supported schools and colleges, is not clear, but it would be a reckless student editor who deliberately tested the law in this area. Hence it's a good idea for school and college editors to develop their sense of libel dangers early.

For the newspaper, the best protections against libel judgments are accuracy and fairness. Sometimes, however, these are not enough. A story may be superficially accurate but basically false, superficially fair but fundamentally prejudicial.

For example, a story might report, with literal accuracy, that a resident assistant in a dormitory disappeared shortly after the discovery of thefts from a number of rooms. While true on the surface, these words might be basically false, and therefore libelous, because of their implication that the assistant took off when it appeared that he was about to be exposed as a thief.

Although as a practical matter a statement is not libelous if it is true in word and implication, the copyreader must remember that the burden of proof is on the publisher, not on the person alleging libel. In other words, if a case comes to trial, the plaintiff need not show that the defamatory statement is false; all he need do is convince the jury that the statement is defamatory and that it was made by the defendant, the publisher. Once he has done that, the publisher must either prove that the statement is true or show that he had legal justification, other than truth, for printing it.

Because the law puts this burden of proof on the publisher, the copyreader must be sure that potentially libelous statements are not merely true but provably true as well. He may be convinced that Smith is telling the truth when he calls Jones a liar, but if he fears that Smith won't be willing to testify, or that in the event of a trial it will be just Smith's word against Jones' or that Jones can recruit convincing witnesses to testify in his behalf, he had better not let the accusation get into print.

This hypothetical case points up another problem: reporters sometimes have a misconception of what constitutes truth. In this instance, the reporter might argue that Smith did call Jones a liar, that there are witnesses willing to testify that he did so, that it is therefore provably true that Smith spoke the words, and that the paper is therefore legally safe in reporting that he said it. But the reporter would be wrong. In such cases the test of truth must be applied not to the fact of utterance of the words but to the validity of the words uttered. The paper would therefore have to prove that Jones is a liar, and that, obviously, would be harder than proving that Smith *called* Jones a liar.

A libel is the legal responsibility not only of the person who originates it but also of anyone who repeats it. This principle can restrain a newspaper from publishing a statement, however newsworthy, that damages reputation. Whether a comment is made in a speech, an interview, a letter to the editor, or an advertisement, it is potentially dangerous to the person who publishes it. The Montgomery, Alabama, officials' suits against *The New York Times*, for example, were based not on material from the *Times'* news or editorial columns but on an advertisement paid for by persons having no connection with the newspaper.

An honest mistake does not excuse a libel, nor does the publication of a correction, retraction, or apology release the publisher from liability. A newspaper might report that Hercules Poltroon has been suspended from the university for violation of the honor system, on complaint of Atlas Defrost, and then learn to its dismay that a careless reporter had reversed the names. Poltroon has a case, even if the error was inadvertent and the paper runs a correction promptly and prominently and humbly.

Proof that a libel was unintentional, or that a retraction was published, can be evidence that the publisher acted in good faith and can lessen the amount of the judgment awarded to the plaintiff. Such a showing may, in addition, put a burden on the plaintiff to prove that he actually was damaged, and to what extent, monetarily. Three types of damages can be awarded in a libel case: "general damages," which are assumed from the fact of the libel, need not be proved by the plaintiff, and can be fixed at the discretion of the jury; "special damages" or actual injury that can and must be proved (loss of wages or customers or contracts, for example); and "punitive damages," which are assessed by the jury to punish the libeler, usually when it is convinced that the libel was published deliberately and with intent to injure. In some states, the law specifies that if a libelous statement is adequately corrected or retracted the plaintiff cannot collect general or punitive damages, but must limit his claim to special or actual damage.

In practice, most persons who believe themselves to have been injured by inaccurate newspaper reporting are satisfied with a correction or retraction, and press their complaints no further. Nevertheless, sloppy reporting is dangerous, and the copyreader should be sure that facts have been verified and identifications clearly established. Police stories are particularly troublesome. A teetotaling pillar of virtue may have the same name as a barfly who spends the night in the town drunk tank. The copyreader who handles the story of the arrest should make sure the story includes all the details that make the identification clear—full name including middle initial, age, address, and sometimes occupation. (Persons who get involved, by chance, in spot news such as accidents, fires and rescues sometimes object bitterly to having their ages used. The libel hazard isn't the only reason for ignoring their protests, but it can be one of them.)

The possibility of libel should not make the editor timid, for the paper that is sure of its facts and fair to persons in the news runs little danger. Nor must the newspaper always be ready to prove the truth of whatever it publishes, from whatever source. Some material is "privileged" and may be used regardless of truth.

The doctrine of privilege can be complex, but basically it concerns the circumstances under which a statement is made or a record set down. In general, privilege attaches to words spoken or written in the official conduct of public business. The doctrine is based on the democratic theory that the public interest demands unfettered debate of public issues, and that at times the individual's right to protection of reputation must be subordinated to the public's right to know about the workings of government, the actions of governmental officials, and the fortunes of private citizens who deal with public agencies. The principle finds expression in Article I Section 6 of the United States Constitution, which provides that members of Congress "shall not be questioned in any other place"—that is, subjected to legal action—"for any speech or debate in either House."

Senators and representatives are said to have "absolute privilege" when they are on the floor or sitting formally in committee. They cannot be arrested or sued or otherwise called to account, except by the electorate at the polls, for anything they say there. By extension—through statute, judicial interpretation, and custom—other officials at federal, state, and local levels have similar protection, although in lesser degree, when they are carrying out their official duties.

Privilege is important to the newsman because the doctrine's protection extends to him and his publication when he is reporting the privileged statements and records of public officials. If, from the floor of the House, a congressman defames a colleague, or another public official, or a private citizen, he has absolute privilege and runs no risk of losing a lawsuit. And the reporter in the press gallery may include the defamatory comments in his story without risking a damage judgment. He and the copyreader must remember, however, that his privilege, unlike the speaker's, is not absolute. It is qualified, or conditional, in that he has full protection only if his story is accurate, fair, impartial, and published in good faith, without malice. The speaker, having absolute privilege, can misquote a colleague and get away with it, but the reporter who misquotes the speaker does so at his peril. Inaccurate, unfair, or malicious stories are not protected by privilege.

The copyreader must remember that the test for privilege is twofold: the occasion or record must be "official" and it must be "public." Either condition alone may not be enough. Suppose the mayor calls the police chief to his office and orders him to have a detective follow a city councilman and try to catch the councilman taking horse race bets. The order is official enough, but it's not public, and if a reporter has overheard it from the hallway, and writes a story about it, he may not be successful in claiming privilege should the councilman sue him and his newspaper for libel.

Similarly, if a soapbox orator in the town square accuses a department store owner of dishonesty and discriminatory practices, his remarks are highly public but hardly official, and the editor had better not assume that a story about the accusation is privileged.

On the other hand, the newspaper is safe in reporting proceedings of the state legislature and the courts, as long as the stories are fair and accurate, in reporting what goes on at city council or school board meetings, as long as the comments quoted are relevant to the public business, and in quoting councilmen, school directors, county commissioners, medical examiners, district attorneys, judges, coroners, and the like, provided their remarks are a reasonable exercise of their responsibilities as public officials.

That's a large "provided that." Both reporter and editor should be aware that the lower one goes in the governmental structure, and the fewer and less formal and dignified the trappings of official proceedings become, the less likely are the courts to recognize privilege as a defense. For example, privilege would unquestionably attach to a fair and accurate report of anything said by the President of the United States, even if the President were dealing unfairly and inaccurately with as trivial a topic as the table manners of a minor White House functionary. But if a township committeeman should attack the table manners of one of the community's volunteer firemen, the privilege would be questionable. Even if the committeeman made the remarks openly at a public meeting of the township committee, the newspaper might have to prove that the comments were relevant to the public business. Failing that, it would have to fall back on the more difficult defense of truth.

Police and court proceedings, both criminal and civil, often raise questions of privilege. The safest and fairest procedure in criminal matters is to stick to the public record. If a man is charged with burglary, the newspaper is safe in saying so because the legal papers, as public records, are privileged. Until a charge has been filed in writing, however, it is usually sound practice not to identify the suspect. For one thing, to report that a person is suspected of a crime is in itself damaging. If a man is picked up for questioning in a child-molesting case, for example, his friends and neighbors will reason that he has given the police some cause to suspect him, and even if he is completely cleared his reputation may be tarnished forever. For another, police sometimes change their minds, and it can be risky to report that charges "will be filed." Local traditions, judicial attitudes, and police-press relationships help determine the newspaper's policy in such circumstances, but the copyreader should nevertheless remember that until there is a formal record there is no privilege.

Civil actions—lawsuits—can also cause problems. In some states, the plaintiff's complaint, or statement of his cause of action and the relief he seeks, is privileged from the moment it is filed with the clerk of court, and can safely be reported in detail. In others, conditional privilege does not apply until a judge has taken judicial notice of the suit, through ruling on a preliminary motion, or issuing a "show cause" order, or taking some other action which shows that the suit has actually entered the court machinery. In such jurisdictions it has been held, in effect, that the absolute right of an individual to bring legal action against another does not give a third party the right to repeat the accusations made in the complaint—until the charge has become part of a court proceeding.

In addition to recognizing conditional privilege, the law regards "fair comment" as a proper defense in libel actions. The principle here is that anything offered for public approval may be criticized freely as long as the criticism is based on fact, is not malicious, and represents the honest opinion of the critic.

Thus a newspaper may criticize a public official, artist, athlete, writer, singer, actress, musician, dancer, or any other performer. The criticism may be exceedingly caustic and still not exceed the limits of fair comment, provided it involves the person's public performance and not his private character. A reviewer may safely write that a singer's voice is hoarse and offkey, but if he says the voice shows the effects of too much alcohol he'd better be ready to produce some proof.

In its comments on public officials and "public figures," the press is allowed great latitude, and to the extent that private character and conduct affect an officeholder's fitness for office the press may go beyond the limitations imposed on its criticism of persons in other fields. Court decisions of the 1960s held that even untruthful comments about public officials could not be a basis for damages if the comments were not malicious, "recklessly false," or known by the publisher to be false. "Public figures" in this context means persons who do not hold public office but who have placed themselves in a position in which their activities are so mixed with those of public interest that discussion of their activities is considered more important than their right to protection from unfair publicity. Thus the United States Supreme Court ruled that a retired Army general who remained in the public eye as a private citizen was a "public figure." The Supreme Court of the state of Washington ruled similarly in the case of a basketball coach at a state university. As a public figure, neither the general nor the coach was entitled to the same protection, under the libel law, that was accorded private citizens.

In a landmark decision in 1971, the United States Supreme Court extended the public official-public figure doctrine to cover private citizens who are involved in matters of public concern. Thus, when the public interest is involved, the "private" person must prove malice—deliberate or reckless falsity—before being entitled to a judgment for libel.

In most circumstances, the copy editor does not have the final word on whether or not to use potentially libelous material. But he has an obligation to be aware of the libel hazard and to call questionable passages to the attention of the responsible editor.

Aside from considerations of legal responsibility, the ethical newspaper wants to be fair. It does not impute guilt to a suspect. It does not publish one side of a controversy without trying to present the other. It gives a person or an institution that is under attack the chance to reply. When it makes a mistake it acknowledges the error, without equivocating.

The greatest of all of the copyreader's responsibilities is to make certain that every story is fair.

Pitfalls

THE copyreader should be like the defensive driver, watching what the other fellow does, anticipating what he will do wrong, looking for the signals that tell him of extra danger.

Names, numbers, and dates are warning lights, and the editor who doesn't stop for them is courting trouble.

Reporters do odd things with names. They misspell them. They get the middle initial wrong. They leave out "Jr." when it's needed and put it in when it's not. They leave out first names. They mix up the miss and the matron. They transpose, so that Smith becomes Jones and Jones becomes Smith. They change Jack to John when the correct name is really Jack.

The copyreader is not obliged to check every name himself. But he should be suspicious, and should check if he has any doubt. The experienced copyreader has a sixth sense about names, particularly those in his own community. He is particularly wary of names that have varied spellings: Kelly, Kelley; Green, Greene; Klein, Kline; McKay, MacKay, Mackay; Lee, Lea, Leigh, Li; Shafer, Shaffer, Schafer, Schaffer, Schaefer, Schaeffer. He questions those that just don't look like names: Henry Pingpong, Irving Cuttlefish. He doesn't necessarily accept the reporter's assurance that the name is right. He uses the phone book, or *Who's Who in America*, or a student directory, or some other reliable source book. He'll still miss a few. But the important thing is that he challenge every name that he doubts. He should act on his hunches, not by changing a spelling on the basis of guesswork, but by asking about it. He should realize that it's easy for a reporter to switch names around. If Black and Green disagree, Black's argument may come out as Green's and Green's as Black's. Once the reporter has made the error, he's not likely to catch it himself.

The editor should view numbers as the young view their elders: with deep suspicion. The lead on a story about a college election said that Ed

Leary beat Sam Kitzenberg by 819 votes. The third paragraph said the vote was Leary 1,223, Kitzenberg 304. Something wrong there.

The lead of another story referred to 39 paintings in a traveling art exhibition. Later, the story said there were five paintings from each of the states of Arizona, Idaho, Montana, New Mexico, Utah, and Wyoming, and four from Colorado. Something wrong there, too.

The copyreader couldn't know offhand whether Leary won by 919 votes (not 819), or whether Leary polled 1,123 votes (not 1,223), or whether Kitzenberg polled 404 votes (not 304). He couldn't know whether there were 34 paintings in the exhibition (not 39), or whether the story should have listed eight states (not seven). So he couldn't make changes without checking with someone. He would go to the reporter first. If he couldn't find the reporter, he would call an election official about the first story, and the chairman of the art department about the second. What he would not do is let the inconsistency remain in the copy.

An inconsistency can be hard to spot, as it is here:

```
     A candidate for the position of
Daily Evergreen editor stepped out of
the race to provide the Publications
Board with its quorum for an editorial
choice yesterday.
     The absence of members Roger Shelton
and Matthew Carey made a vote impossible.
Carol Mortland provided the necessary
extra vote by relinquishing her candidacy
for Daily Evergreen editor thus giving
the board their necessary two-thirds
quorum of eight.
```

This passage is so jumbled that the copyreader should have been on the alert for factual error. He wasn't, though; the story was published just this way. The inconsistency in the arithmetic is this: if a quorum of eight constitutes two-thirds of the board, the board must have twelve members. According to the story, only two were absent. That would have provided ten votes, or nine with Miss Mortland abstaining. Yet it allegedly took Miss Mortland's vote to provide eight votes. Hence there must have been two other absentees besides Shelton and Carey. So the reporter erred in reporting the size of the quorum required, or he was protecting a couple of board members, or he was doing a hatchet job on Shelton and Carey. In any case, the copyreader should have acted.

Most difficult to spot are casual numerical inconsistencies. The second paragraph of a story on a Supreme Court decision reported that the vote was 8–1. Many paragraphs later it was noted that one justice did not take part. Hence the vote had to have been either 8–0 or 7–1. Because the two references were so widely separated in the story, however, the inconsistency was hard to spot.

Here is another tricky type of error, taken from a story about a school board meeting:

```
     Amundsen said he planned to
recommend that pupils in grades
3-6 attend Packer School next year,
while children in kindergarten and
grades 1-3 attend Perkins.
```

The overlap at grade 3 is kind of sneaky.

Numbers in the hundreds of thousands, millions, and billions can slide by with undetected errors. An example:

```
     Mr. Charlo said, "As an example,
we asked Dean Rusk why people in the
United States are starving, and pointed
out to him that the amount of money
spent in one month to fight the war
in Vietnam is the same amount of money
allocated to the poverty program for
the entire year — $2 million."
```

A second's thought would have told the copyreader that the number had to be billion, not million, but he read right over it. Another copyreader read right over a reference to an 18,000,000-acre state prison farm. Big prison farm, that; approximately the size of Belgium. Three extra zeros in the number, probably.

Although there may not be much he can do about it, the copyreader should be suspicious of crowd figures, even for small crowds. When ten students were asked to estimate the crowd at a lecture, they gave these reports: "large," "small," "moderate-sized," "more than 300," "about 300," "about 500," "about 400," "350," "250," and "nearly 400."

If a count of a confined audience can produce such varied results, it is clear that estimates of the throngs at parades, political rallies, and street riots are not to be trusted, either. About all the copyreader can do, though, is see that the story gives a source for the estimate so that the reader will have some gauge of its reliability, or lack of it.

The same holds for estimates of losses from fires and other disasters. Persons who have a financial interest may give distorted figures, either deliberately or because their interest distorts their judgment. The story should note whether the source of an estimate is an owner, an insurance adjuster, or a fire chief.

Dates, too, should stop the copyreader momentarily. It's easy to err in a computation. One of the easiest errors to spot, and one of the most frequently unspotted, is the inconsistency between birth date and age. Undertakers and reporters sometimes just subtract the year of birth from the year of death. But a man who was born on November 3, 1920, is not 50 years old on April 30, 1970. He's still 49. The copyreader should *always* make this computation. And in handling obituaries he should remember that the undertaker, the usual source of obituary data, may be the type who reports that a client died "in his 59th year." That usually means the client is 58, but sometimes he really is 59.

In addition to watching the other fellow, the copyreader must check his own habits. He must remember that when he changes language he may be changing meaning, that when he reorganizes he may be deleting an essential fact, and that when he edits one part of a story he may be creating a need for editing elsewhere. He should therefore review his editing before he sends his story on. If he has made more than routine changes, he should consciously ask himself these questions:

(1) Have I changed the facts?
(2) Have I knocked out anything essential?
(3) Have I made the story as a whole conform to the editing I have done?

Let's look at one story, a hypothetical one this time, in which the editing involves all three of these dangers:

```
        The trial of G. Franklin Kazoo
came to an end today in Adams County
Common Pleas Court.
        A jury of 7 men and 5 women de-
liberated for two hours before re-
turning their verdict to Judge
Howard Contempt.
        They found Kazoo, 43-year-old
itinerant berry picker from Apathy
```

Falls, New Hampshire, guilty of first degree murder in the shotgun death of Murphy Champagne, 28, another berry picker, in a tenant farmhouse near Millville last September 23.

Judge Contempt sentenced Kazoo to life imprisonment in the state penitentiary at Rockport.

Kazoo didn't show any emotion at the verdict or the sentence, but sang "Bringing in the Sheaves" as he was led from the courtroom. His court appointed defense council, Warren J. Brier, said there would be no appeal.

Prosecutor Lyle Harris charged during the three-day trial that Kazoo shot Champagne in a dispute over a gambling debt.

Kazoo admitted on the stand that he had cautioned Champagne with a

12-gauge shotgun, but testified that he meant only to frighten him. "The gun went off accidentally."

Another berry picker, Donald C. Miller, testified he heard two men arguing in the barn and then heard a shot, after which he rushed in and found Champagne on the floor and Kazoo standing nearby with a shotgun in his hands.

There are real problems in this story, and the copyreader must make many alterations. First, of course, he must make the lead say something. That entails reorganization, and reorganization creates additional problems. Here is what he does first:

~~The trial of~~ G. Franklin Kazoo was convicted of ~~came to an end today in Adams County Common Pleas Court~~.

~~A jury of 7 men and 5 women deliberated for two hours before returning their verdict to Judge Howard Contempt~~.

~~They found Kazoo, 43-year-old itinerant berry picker from Apathy Falls, New Hampshire, guilty of~~ first degree murder today in the shotgun.

death of Murphy Champagne~~, 28,~~ ~~another berry picker,~~ in a tenant farmhouse near Millville last ~~Sep-tember~~ Sept. 23.

Judge Contempt sentenced Kazoo to life imprisonment in the state penitentiary at Rockport.

Kazoo ~~didn't show any~~ showed no emotion at the verdict or the sentence, but sang "Bringing in the Sheaves" as he was led from the courtroom. His court-appointed defense ~~council,~~ counsel, Warren J. Brier, said there would be no appeal.

Prosecutor Lyle Harris charged during the three-day trial that Kazoo shot Champagne in a dispute over a gambling debt.

Kazoo admitted on the stand that he had ~~cautioned~~ threatened Champagne with a 12-gauge shotgun, but testified that he meant only to frighten him. "The gun went off accidentally," he said.

```
    Another berry picker, Donald C.

Miller, testified he heard two men

arguing in the ~~barn~~ farmhouse and then heard

a shot. ~~after which~~ He rushed in, he said, and

found Champagne on the floor and Kazoo

standing nearby with a shotgun in his hands.
                            #
```

Note that in making the lead say something the copyreader has created a number of new problems. He has deleted the place of trial, the makeup of the jury, the length of the deliberation, the age, occupation, and home town of the defendant, the age and occupation of the victim, and the first name of the judge. He must get these elements back in. One way is to cut the story apart after the second or third paragraph (of the edited version) and paste in the information, either typewritten or in longhand. Although typing would be better for legibility, we'll do it in longhand here in order to make the procedure stand out a little better:

```
    ~~The trial of~~ G. Franklin Kazoo
was convicted of
~~came to an end today in Adams County~~

~~Common Pleas Court.~~

    ~~A jury of 7 men and 5 women de-~~

~~liberated for two hours before re-~~

~~turning their verdict to Judge~~

~~Howard Contempt.~~

    ~~They found Kazoo, 43-year-old~~

~~itinerant berry picker from Apathy~~

~~Falls, New Hampshire, guilty of~~

first degree murder today in the shotgun
```

death of Murphy Champagne~~, 28,~~

~~another berry picker,~~ in a tenant

farmhouse near Millville last ~~Sep-~~

Sept.
~~tember~~ 23.

Howard
Judge Contempt sentenced Kazoo

to life imprisonment in the state

penitentiary at Rockport.

showed no
Kazoo ~~didn't show any~~ emotion

at the verdict or the sentence, but

sang "Bringing in the Sheaves" as he

was led from the courtroom. His

counsel,
court=appointed defense ~~council,~~

Warren J. Brier, said there would

be no appeal.

The jury of seven men and
five women deliberated for two
hours before returning its verdict
in Adams County Common Pleas Court.

Kazoo, 43, is an itinerant berry
picker from Apathy Falls, N.H. Champagne
also was a berry picker. He was
28.

Prosecutor Lyle Harris charged during the three-day trial that Kazoo shot Champagne in a dispute over a gambling debt.

Kazoo admitted on the stand that he had ~~cautioned~~ threatened Champagne with a 12-gauge shotgun, but testified that he meant only to frighten him. "The gun went off accidentally," he said.

Another berry picker, Donald C. Miller, testified he heard two men arguing in the ~~barn~~ farmhouse and then heard a shot. ~~after which~~ He rushed in, he said, and found Champagne on the floor and Kazoo standing nearby with a shotgun in his hands.

#

One step remains: to read the story over a final time, checking for omissions and repetition.

Cutlines

CUTLINES vary in design. They are usually set in type somewhat larger than the body type. Some papers set cutlines in lightface, some in bold, some in light italic. Some indent at the left, some indent on both sides, some use paragraph form, and some like a "hanging indentation" with the top line flush and other lines indented. Some set lines in one block, to the measure of the picture, but most divide the lines into two or more columns when they are carried under wide pictures.

Some offices use the caption, which is a short descriptive phrase that can be set as a title or a headline, essentially separate from the rest of the cutlines, or as an introductory phrase that is part of the cutlines. If the caption is used as a title or a headline, it is set in larger and bolder type than the cutlines, and is carried above them centered or left flush, or above the picture as an "overline." If the caption simply introduces the cutlines, it is usually set in capitals or boldface or both. It can be either a phrase or a label, set apart from the rest of the cutlines by a dash or a colon, or it can be handled as a boldface lead-in, an integral part of the cutline sentence structure, but set in a different typeface.

Here are some examples of cutline style:

Photo by Howard Guenther

David Long, graduate assistant in Plant Physiology, examines his soy beans in one of the environmental growth chambers located in the Botany and Zoology Building. Long's plants are given 12 hours of light and 12 hours of darkness under controlled temperature conditions.

(UPI Telephoto)

It's Back Again

Big and square, elegant and ugly, this 1907 Thomas Flyer goes thru toll gate on San Francisco-Oakland Bay bridge en route to San Francisco to finish cross-country trip much as it did when it first rolled into town 60 years ago.

Let's All Go Home

Kenneth and Carol Villaros had their hands full yesterday when they left a hospital in Santa Monica with their quadruplet sons. The babies, born June 1, are Gary Lee, Stephen Lee, Kevin Lee and Kenneth Lee. The slightly perplexed looking girl on right, who is holding hands with little brother Kenneth, is the Villaros' other child, Stefanie, $3^1/_2$.

MOSQUITOES WILL BITE THE DUST when Malcolm Soare wings over the city in this plane spreading Baytex, a mosquito spray which is non-toxic to humans and animals. Soare will be spraying about three times during the summer and will be flying at altitudes of 100 to 200 feet. In the photo, Soare is flushing out the tank of the spray plane preparatory to filling it with the mosquito spray.

THE SUBJECT WAS WATER: Governor Rockefeller and, from the left, Secretary of the Interior Stewart L. Udall, Gov. Raymond P. Schafer of Pennsylvania and Gov. Richard J. Hughes of New Jersey at meeting of the Delaware River Basin Commission yesterday.

LONER *hikes through dense Huckleberry Mountain forest near Hunters, Wash., surrounded by creations bearing little likeness to freeways.* (S-R)

—Associated Press Wirephoto

CONFRONTATION IN COPENHAGEN

COPENHAGEN—Charlotte Ohrvald, 1, points with joy and surprise to guard outside Amalienborg Castle. Small wonder, he's her father, Jens Ohrvald. She was taken for a stroll near the palace where many Danish citizens walk to seek news of Princess Margrethe who is expecting her first child sometime this month.

BACK FROM HARD LUCK VOYAGE—Sitting in dinghy at Marina Del Rey are members of the Jastram family, from left, Forrest, 2, Alesia, 5, Robert Jastram and a young friend, Stanley Hurd, 13. On their disabled trimaran are Mrs. Jastram with Lance, 13, and Portland, 4.

Times photo by Joe Kennedy

Governors Open 60th Convention

Governors attending the 60th National Governors' Conference pose Monday for the photo, at the convention hall in Cincinnati. Chairman John A. Volpe, governor of Massachusetts, is standing. Others seated at head of table are, from left: Gov. Raymond Shafer of Pennsylvania; Ohio Gov. James A. Rhodes, host; and Gov. Charles L. Terry Jr. of Delaware. (AP photo)

—Associated Press Wirephoto

The warmth of a welcome for President Johnson in El Salvador on Saturday was marred by a group of protesting students who spattered his limousine with paint. The Secret Service agents on the car are shown reacting as an egg splattered and spread all over the car.

Ex-Chief's Villa Raided

The house belonging to the son of the deposed former Czech president, Antonin Novotny, center, raided by burglars Sunday night, resulted in damage estimated at $3,000. Novotny and his son, Antonin Jr., right, talk to a newsman Monday outside the villa near Prague. This is the first photo of Novotny since he was deposed early this year by the new liberal regime. (AP photo)

New Haight Violence

Police arrested this suspected bottle thrower atop a building

Whatever the design, cutlines are usually brief and in the present tense. Years ago, perhaps in the belief that some readers would look at the picture and cutlines but not read the accompanying story, the lines often told the whole story themselves. Modern practice, however, is to limit the cutlines to an explanation of what is in the picture, and even then to ignore elements of the picture that are self-explanatory.

In the old style, a football picture might have had these underlines:

> OFF AND RUNNING — Eddie Sooperbach, Central High halfback (No. 42 in white jersey at left, with ball, indicated by arrow), swings around his own right end at the start of a 76-yard touchdown jaunt against Vocational yesterday on the Central High field while an unidentified blocker, right, clears two Indian players from his path under the eye of head linesman Tony Ramunni (extreme right, in striped shirt). Despite Sooperbach's heroics, Vocational won the game, 72-6, for its 24th consecutive victory, sixth straight this season, and 34th in a row over Central.

Today, the lines would go more like this:

> Eddie Sooperbach of Central swings around end at the start of his 76-yard touchdown run against Vocational.

If the picture were carried "cutlines only," with no accompanying story, the lines would note who won, where the game was played, and perhaps a few other details.

Because cutlines are written in the present tense, describing what "is" going on in the picture, they do not normally include a time factor. When the time element is included, it is usually in possessive form or in a separate sentence, so that it does not cause an awkward clash of tenses.

This is awkward:

> TIRED OF IT ALL — Casey, the 756-pound male gorilla of the Como Zoo in St. Paul, Minn., indulges in a wide yawn yesterday as sedation began to wear off after his flight to the Henry Doorly Zoo in Omaha, Neb., where, officials hope, he will mate successfully with the Omaha zoo's two female gorillas.

These are better:

> TIRED OF IT ALL — Casey, the 756-pound male gorilla of the Como Zoo in St. Paul, Minn., <u>yawns</u> as sedation <u>begins</u> to wear off after his flight to the Henry Doorly Zoo in Omaha, Neb. Casey was sent to Omaha yesterday to try the mating game with two female gorillas there.

> TIRED OF IT ALL — Casey, the 756-pound male gorilla of the Como Zoo in St. Paul, Minn., <u>yawns</u> as sedation <u>begins</u> to wear off after <u>yesterday's</u> flight to the Henry Doorly Zoo in Omaha, Neb. Officials hope he will mate successfully with the Omaha zoo's two female gorillas.

The copyreader who handles the cutlines does not always get a look at the picture, but when he does he should make sure the lines are consistent with what he sees. It's too bad to have cutlines identify three people when there are only two in the picture.

It is ideal for the copyreader who handles the cutlines to handle the accompanying story. The practice helps avoid inconsistencies like this one, taken from a newspaper:

(cutlines) The third hole proved Jack Nicklaus' undoing in Thursday's round of the Akron Classic. His second shot buried in the mud of a lake bank and he had to remove one shoe and one sock and stand in 15 inches of water in order to blast the ball out. In this graphic series of pictures you see Jack taking off the shoe, heading for the water, ready for the shot, and drying off his foot. The ball carried over the green and Jack three-putted.

(story) Nicklaus ran into trouble on No. 3. His second shot landed on the edge of a pond but was playable. Jack took off his shoes and socks, stepped into the water and hit out of the mud. He still needed three more strokes to get down and the double-bogey six cost him a chance of breaking par.

The careful copyreader would note two inconsistencies here. The obvious one is the matter of how many shoes and socks came off. The other is the question of Nicklaus' score on the hole. The story says he took a six, but the burden of the cutlines is that he took a seven. (If the third shot "carried over the green," as reported, he presumably needed one to get back before taking his three putts.)

Cutlines entail the same writing problems as other copy. Here's some stammering:

> BALL CLOBBERS BASE RUNNER — Ball bounces
> away from Cleveland Indians' second baseman
> Dave Nelson after hitting him in the back as
> he slid into third base after advancing from
> first on a single to center by Pitcher Sam
> McDowell in the fifth inning at Yankee Stadium
> in New York yesterday. The throw by Yankee
> center fielder Joe Pepitone hit Nelson, but
> he remained in the game.

The first sentence, nearly 50 words long, is incomprehensibly cluttered. The lines say three times that the ball hit the runner, and they have an awkward combination of past and present tenses. They could be improved by this editing:

> BALL CLOBBERS BASE RUNNER — The ~~B~~ball bounces
> away from Cleveland Indians' second baseman
> Dave Nelson after hitting him in the back as
> he slides ~~slid~~ into third base in yesterday's game against the New York Yankees ~~after advancing from~~
> Nelson advanced from first on a single ~~to center~~ by Pitcher Sam
> McDowell in the fifth inning ~~at Yankee Stadium~~
> in New York. ~~yesterday. The throw by~~ Yankee
> center fielder Joe Pepitone made the throw ~~hit Nelson, but~~
> to third.
> ~~he remained in the game.~~

Sometimes it is necessary to carry a picture on one page and its story on another. The cutlines should then include a notation like this: *(Story on Page 14.)* The story should carry a similar reference to the picture, at the start or finish or as an insert, in a typeface that differs from the body type.

Most newspapers carry "credit lines" to identify the photographer or the agency responsible for the picture. The most common style is an agate line carried flush right between the cut and the cutlines.

Cutlines often get slapdash treatment at the copy desk. They shouldn't. They are as much a part of the editorial product as stories, editorials, pictures, and heads, and should be treated with as much respect.

Headlines

THE best way to start writing headlines is to start thinking in headline language.

The head is written in telegraphic form, usually in the present tense, usually without the articles "a," "an," and "the," and often with a comma or a semicolon substituting for the conjunction "and." It frequently drops an auxiliary verb and sometimes has no verb at all.

The aspiring copyreader can warm up for headwriting by thinking about the scenes around him in "headline sentences" like these:

```
Late Risers Hurry to Dining Hall

Alert Meter Maid Tickets Car

Coed Trips on Steps, Pretends Nothing Happened

Thirsty Scholar Discouraged by Line at Fountain

Professor Bores Class

Movie Is Terrible, Viewer Believes

Windows Rattled by Sonic Boom
```

Writing a headline is harder than composing a headline sentence, but every head originates with an idea like this. The experienced deskman summarizes a story as he copyreads, and when he turns to the head he generally has a headline sentence already in mind.

The headline is a story's packaging and is important to the appearance and character of the newspaper. Different offices have different tastes. Whether you'll write "LBJ Likes HHH in Race with Dick" or "Johnson Predicts Humphrey Will Win" will depend pretty much on the tone your paper wants to set.

Copy desks differ both in their choice of language and in their philosophy of what the headline ought to be. In this century, the traditional headline has told the basic facts of the story. It has gone to the main point; it has looked for the news. In recent years, however, there has been a trend toward the "label" headline, a magazine type of head that hints at the story's content but sets the scene or the mood more than it sets forth facts.

Whereas news heads might read "Subzero Weather Forecast" and "Survivor Tells of Shipwreck," label heads might say "Earmuff Time Ahead" and "Delirium and Death at Sea."

The label head has become more popular as the newspaper has become more streamlined, dropping its column rules, widening columns, varying type sizes and measures, weighting Page One on the left side, centering heads, and deviating in other ways from the dominant makeup concepts of the first half of the century. Actually, though, the label is the more conservative of the headline styles, for it was in widespread use before the news head became popular late in the nineteenth century. When Abraham Lincoln was shot, for example, the top deck of *The New York Times* headline did not say "President Shot." It said "Awful Event."

Regardless of a paper's approach to the news or its concept of the function of the headline, the head must be well constructed or the appearance of the paper will suffer.

To be passable, a headline must be accurate, informative, and grammatical.

To be good, it should also:

- Reflect the main point or idea of the story
- Include as much information as possible
- Be forceful
- Come to the point quickly
- Please the eye
- Be in good taste and reflect the mood of the story
- Have a subject, in the grammatical sense
- Avoid splitting grammatical units from one line to the next
- Avoid padding
- Avoid "headlinese"
- Flow as one sentence.

Factual and grammatical accuracy can be hard to come by. The headwriter is restricted by space; he must say a lot in a few words. Under compulsion to compress, he may say more than the story says, or imply something that is not in the story, or say too little, or miss the point, or cut a grammatical corner.

Under pressure of a deadline he may misread a story or, to fit the headline to the space, he may juggle language in such a way that he misplaces the emphasis.

Whether he is writing a label or a news headline, in formal or informal language, he should base the head on the main point of a story, not on secondary material. If the lead says the police found a new clue, and the seventh paragraph says someone is under arrest for the crime, it's logical to assume that the arrest was reported earlier. The head should deal with the new clue, not the arrest.

The secret to getting as much information as possible into the headline is brevity, and this means brevity of word as well as of phrase. If the copyreader uses "prohibition" when "ban" would do the job, or if he is repetitious or uses unnecessary detail, he's missing a chance to get more information into the head.

The headwriter achieves force the same way the reporter does—by using meaningful, active verbs. That doesn't mean the passive isn't acceptable or even preferable when usage dictates ("Man Hurt in Fall," for example, is more natural than "Fall Hurts Man"). But the headwriter should use the active voice as much as possible, and avoid the flabby verb "to be."

A head should come to the point by opening with facts that make the story a story, rather than by emphasizing words that could apply equally to other stories. There is nothing really wrong with a headline that reads "President Says/Peace Is Near." But the President is always saying things, and the news is not *that* he says but *what* he says. So this is better: "Peace is Near,/President Says." For the same reason, "Traffic Crash/Kills Three men" is not as strong a head as "Three Men Killed/In Traffic Crash," even though it is in the active voice.

To be pleasing to the eye, the length of the lines should not vary greatly and should not leave too much white space. The modern trend to the left flush head has given the headwriter more freedom than he used to have because flush heads should be a bit ragged at the right side, whereas the old-fashioned "stepline" head, in which the top line is flush left and the bottom flush right, looks sloppy if the lines are uneven. But excessive variation in length makes a flush head unattractive. Because of differences in type and headline design there can be no inflexible rule, but for most purposes a variation of no more than two units between the longest line and the shortest is a reasonable goal.

Good taste is a matter of subjective judgment. The headwriter won't go wrong, though, if he matches the tone of the headline with the facts of the story, and avoids making light of misfortune or doing intentional hurt. Injury should be reported by the facts of the story, not inflicted by the way they are presented. A lot of readers would take exception to this headline, which a daily newspaper carried on a story about a fatal explosion: "Six Men Blown/To Smithereens." And to this one, over a story about death in a recreation hall that was swept away in a flash flood: "Poker Players Cash in Chips." And the headwriter should never, never ridicule a person by using his name, or his race, or his nationality, or his religion for a play on words.

Heads that have no subject, grammatically speaking, are known as "verb heads." They are generally frowned on because, particularly in the plural form, they can be read as imperatives—orders to do something. The reader who is enjoined to "Arrest Three in Vice Raid" or to "Probe Love Life of Bald Eagle" may answer that it's not his job or that he doesn't want to.

Heads of more than one line should not be broken, from line to line, in such a way as to split logical grammatical units. Among the "don't splits" are:

(1) Names:	Awards Go To Jim Smith, Dick Jones
(2) Titles:	Richards Named Fire Chief of Yogurt City
(3) Name and title:	Mayor Lauds Patrolman Carrington for Rescue
(4) A verb and auxiliary:	Richardson Will Speak at Dinner
(5) Multiword verbs:	Youngster Runs Away from Home
(6) Preposition and object:	Storm Brings Relief to Sweltering City Center
(7) Modifier and the word modified:	Police Seek Fat Man as Suspect
(8) Conjunction and the following word:	Missing Man and Wife Found Safe

In the interest of getting the paper on the street, most offices permit the second line of a three-line head to break on a preposition, and sometimes on a conjunction, and frequently on a modifier. But most disciplined desks bar these splits between the first line and the second, and all other splits regardless of line.

Padding means lengthening a line with unnecessary words simply to fill it out. It takes a variety of forms. One is using an unnecessarily long word, such as "armamentarium" instead of "arsenal." Another is spelling out where an abbreviation or figure is normal, as in "Captain Green" instead of "Capt. Green" or "Fourteen" instead of "14." Still another is using an unnecessary pronoun, as in "Woman Honored on *Her* 100th Birthday." Padding is bad in itself because it robs the language of its punch, but it is particularly undesirable in headlines because it uses space that might otherwise provide additional information.

"Headlinese" is a term that describes unnatural, slangy, or trite language that is found only in headlines, and that is used, generally, only because the space limitations of the headline make it hard for the copyreader to write normally. "Yeggs Bop Cop, Scram with Booze and Boodle" is pure headlinese that, translated, means that safecrackers hit a policeman and then fled with liquor and other loot. Words that are corrupted into other-than-normal meaning, simply for headline purposes, can also be considered headlinese. "Up" and "host" used as verbs are in this category ("Gophers Up Big Ten Lead, Will Host Badgers Saturday"). Unfortunately, such corruptions frequently move from the headline into the rest of the newspaper. As this is written, many sports reporters are treating "host" as a respectable verb. By the time this is read, they may be saying that the Badgers are guesting the Gophers.

In writing the head, the copyreader is restricted mainly by the "unit count," the number of typographical units that fit on a line. The count varies according to the size and measure of the headline type. A 1-column headline in 24-point type has more units than a 1-column head set in 30-point type. A 4-column, 42-point head has more units than a 3-column, 42-point head.

Heads are counted by unit rather than by character because characters vary in width. On typewriters, the key heads are the same size, and the width of any line can therefore be measured by the number of characters in it. That is not true of type. A lower case m is about 50 percent wider than a lower case h, while an upper case M can be four times as wide as a comma or a lower case i.

The width of each character differs from one type family to the next, and the copyreader must adjust his count to the style of type that is used by his publication. A common count is the one used for Bodoni, a type popular in headlines because of its legibility. For headlines set in upper and lower case, Bodoni is counted this way:

All lower case letters *except m, w, f, l, i, and t* count *1 unit*
Lower case m and w count *1½ units*
Lower case f, l, i, and t (*flit*) count *½ unit*
All upper case letters *except M, W, and I* count *1½ units*
Upper case M and W count *2 units*
Upper case I counts *1 unit*
All figures *except 1* count *1½ units*
Figure 1 counts *1 unit*
Fractions count *1½ units*
Symbols ($, %, &) count *1 unit*
Spaces count *½ unit*
Punctuation marks count *½ unit*

Summary

½ unit	*1 unit*	*1½ units*	*2 units*
f l i t	small letters	capital letters	M, W
space	capital I	m, w	
punctuation	figure 1	0, 2 through 9	
	symbols	fractions	

In all-capital heads, now rare, all letters and figures count 1 except M and W (1½) and I and 1 (½). Punctuation marks, spaces, and symbols count ½.

Counting heads can be a laborious job at first. The beginner will move letter by letter, adding as he goes. In the one-line headline "Castro Rations Fuel," he will probably count this way:

C	a	s	t	r	o		R	a	t	i	o	n	s		F	u	e	l
1½	2½	3½	4	5	6	6½	8	9	9½	10	11	12	13	13½	15	16	17	17½

As he gains greater facility, he will develop a technique of looking ahead, compensating for the 1½ counts with ½ counts and vice versa, automatically translating consecutive ½ units into a single count of 1, changing consecutive 1½ units into a single count of 3, and the like. In his mind he will probably move by whole numbers, like this:

C	a	s	t	r	o		R	a	t	i	o	n	s		F	u	e	l
1	2	3	4	5	6	7	8	9		10	11	12	13	14	15	16	17	17½

Every copyreader develops his own counting technique. The secret of speed is practice.

For exercise, you might count the following heads and see whether you get the figure listed. If you don't, try again.

Cemetery Pickets	15½	'Highway Junkies' Urged	22
Ask New Contract	16	To Try Self-Help Club	19½
$10 Billion Cut In Taxes	21½	Rescue Crews Recover	21
Urged By Ford Committee	23	Bodies Of Three Men	19
		Trapped In Mine Blast	20
Cousin's Divorce Scandal	22½		
Puts Queen In Dilemma	20½	U.S. Reviews Farm Policy	23½
		As Food Supplies Dwindle	23

The headwriter's problem, then, is to summarize the story within the limits imposed by (a) the unit count of the head assigned to the story and (b) the rules of grammar and the conventions of headline writing. Unless he is also the managing editor or the news editor or the chief of the copy desk or a combination of these, the copyreader does not usually decide the type of headline that will be put on a story. This is determined for him, so he must be able to write any kind of head on any kind of story.

Papers have different copy desk arrangements and procedures, but most are variants of the system in which the chief of the desk parcels the copy to copyreaders and orders the headlines. The desk chief, whatever his title, is known as the "slotman" because of his traditional position on the inside of the U of a horseshoe desk. If he has responsibilities for makeup—deciding what goes where in the paper or on a given page—he probably decides on the style of headline himself. If he has no makeup responsibilities, as is the case on larger newspapers, he is told what headlines to assign and passes the word along to the copyreaders.

The slotman may describe the head in some detail or use a symbol. In either case, his order specifies the number of lines, the measure in columns or picas, the size of type, the family of type, and the typeface. In detailed instructions, the column measure and type size are usually expressed in numbers divided by a slant bar or dash, while the family and face may be abbreviated. Thus "2 lines 2/36 BBI" means two lines of 36-point Bodoni bold italics, set to 2-column measure. The same headline might also be ordered by the notation "No. 6" or "E" or by some other agreed upon designation. In either case, the copyreader refers to his headline schedule (or his memory, if he has been on the job for a week or so) to determine the count. In the case of 36-point Bodoni bold italics, the maximum count for two 11-pica columns is about 16. The copyreader therefore writes a two-line headline with a unit count ranging between 14 and 16.

His first step is to compose a headline sentence. Suppose he is handling, for the Memorial High School newspaper, a story reporting that Principal Nathan Blumberg has announced the names of 17 students who were named to the first honor roll during the year's third marking period. He tries this headline sentence: "17 Named to Honor Roll." Because it's a two-line head, he divides the sentence this way:

```
17 Named
To Honor Roll
```

Both lines are short, the first counting 9 and the second 12½. So he tries:

```
17 Students Named
To First Honor Roll
```

Now they are too long. The first counts 17, the second 17½. So he tries this:

```
17 Students Win
Scholastic Honors
```

It fits, with a top line of 14½ and a bottom line of 16. The head will do, but it isn't very precise: "scholastic honors" could mean different things. So he keeps trying:

```
First Honor Roll
Lists 17 Students
```

This counts, and it tells the story. But before settling for it he tries some variations to see if they look better:

```
17 at Memorial
Win Top Honors

17 on Honor Roll,
Principal Reports

Honors Won by 17
During Third Period

Third Period Honors
Are Awarded to 17

17 Students Win
Honor Roll Listing

Honor Roll Lists
17 at Memorial
```

There's too much room for individual judgment to say that one of these heads is better than the others. The important thing is that all of them work. Such flexibility of approach is the headwriter's greatest asset. He won't often have to write several headlines on the same story, although it can happen when makeup is adjusted for news developments or changed for new editions, but he must be able to see a variety of approaches to the same headline. If he can't shake loose from the structural approach of the first headline sentence that he tries, he may be in trouble any time his first idea and its variations don't fit the count.

If a head is too long or too short it can often be salvaged by a change in a word or two. The copyreader can change "criticizes" to "raps," "murdered" to "slain," "connected" to "linked," "position" to "post," "opponent" to "foe," "break into" to "raid," "demolish" to "raze" or "wreck," and so on.

But just changing a word doesn't always do the job. There are "long" heads that cannot be easily adjusted because there is no shorter word or phrase that means quite the same thing, or because substitution makes a line too short, or creates a bad break or some other structural fault. So the deskman must be able to shake himself loose from his original idea.

That may mean changing the sentence structure of the headline. For example: a delicatessen owner and a holdup man have exchanged shots. Both have been wounded, and the would-be robber has escaped. The headwriter, faced with a two-liner, maximum count 18, tries the first sentence that comes to him:

```
Store Owner, Robber
Wounded by Gunfire
```

It's close, but the top line counts 19. So he substitutes "thief" for "robber":

```
Store Owner, Thief
Wounded by Gunfire
```

This counts, but the word "thief" doesn't quite catch the meaning. This was more than a simple theft attempt; the headwriter wants to convey the idea of a robbery, a holdup. He considers substituting "Merchant" for "Store Owner" to shorten the top line, but rejects "Merchant" as an archaic word.

So he tries a different kind of identification, making the head read:

```
Robber, Victim Wounded
In Holdup Attempt
```

Since the top line again is too long (21½), he substitutes "Injured" for "Wounded." Still too long (20½). He tries "Hurt." This fits (17½), but he's dissatisfied. The head doesn't get at the idea that this was an attempted holdup of a store. Furthermore, the type of crime involved is conveyed by two words, "robber" and "holdup," so the head is repetitious.

Now he changes his approach. Instead of using a double subject, robber and victim, he emphasizes the victim's role:

```
Store Owner is Shot
After Wounding Robber
```

The second line is too long (20½). Substituting "Shooting" for "Wounding" doesn't help; it means repeating a verb, and the copyreader sees this and doesn't even bother to count. He thinks about changing "Robber" to "Thief," but remembers he has already decided that "thief" and "theft" are inadequate words for this story.

The time has come, he decides, for a major shift in approach. He notes that all the heads he has tried have been in the passive voice. So he changes the construction and uses an active verb:

```
Pistol Shots Wound 2
During Holdup Attempt
```

Both lines are too long (19 and 19½). He tries:

```
Gunshots Wound 2
In Holdup Attempt
```

This fits, but the language implies that both men were attempting the holdup. So he tries still another tack:

```
Store Owner Shoots
Robber, Is Wounded
```

This counts. The lines balance (each is 18). The head has an active verb. It tells the story. There are no bad splits. The copyreader settles for it.

The birth of a head normally does not involve this much pain. An experienced headwriter can often tell without counting that a draft is too long or too short, and he'll sort various possibilities in his mind before he starts writing them down and checking the count. But almost every head can be approached from various directions, as illustrated. If the copyreader finds himself blocked on one route, he backs up and tries another. And if he's really stymied, he puts the head aside, works on something else, and comes back to it later.

Sometimes the specific details of a story just won't fit into the head. This can happen when the facts are complex and the unit count small, or when the story involves names like Wojchiechowicz, Rockefeller, Katzenbach, Turnipseed, and Westmoreland. When he has this problem, the headwriter must try to convey the general idea of the story.

Suppose that at a convention of psychiatrists a speaker has said that "a major unsolved problem" is the chap who isn't really sick but can't control his aggressions. To get these details into a three-line head with a maximum count of 15 is out of the question. But the copyreader can get at the basic idea through generalities:

```
Healthy Patient
Termed Problem
For Psychiatry
```

```
Challenge Seen
In 'Well' Patient
With Hostilities
```

Suppose another speaker has reported that there are 75,000 people in Los Angeles who have tried to commit suicide. The problem in the head is "75,000" because numbers have a high unit count. Here again, working on a three-line head with a 15 count, the solution is the generality:

```
Suicide Termed
Major Problem
In Los Angeles
```

```
Suicide Attempts
Termed Problem
In Los Angeles
```

A complicating element in this story is the need for attribution. It would be much simpler to report the speaker's opinion as fact:

```
75,000 in L.A.
Have Failed in
Suicide Attempts
```

This headline is misleading and editorial, however, for it implies that the speaker's words are above challenge. Often the unit count makes it impossible to identify the speaker, but the head should nevertheless make it clear that someone is being quoted. Among the verb forms that are helpful are "termed," "described as," "viewed as," "held to be," "seen as," "thought to be," and "reported."

Headlines about future events should be written in the future tense. Many offices pay no attention to this rule, but it is one of the most logical. Since the present tense is used in headlines about past events, it is ambiguous to use the present tense for future activities as well. The rule may reasonably be waived for events that are imminent. A story on a football game to be played the day of publication, for example, might be headed "Tigers Face Yale" rather than "Tigers Will Face Yale." But if it's announced that a legislator will give a talk next week, the head should be

```
Sen. Case
Will Speak
On Campus
```

and not

```
Sen. Case
Gives Talk
On Campus
```

And if the story is about a construction project, the head should be

```
New Student Union
To Be Ready in Fall
```

and not

```
New Student Union
Is Ready Next Fall
```

Note that one head says "*Will* Speak" and the other "*To* Be Ready." In most offices, the forms "will" and "to" are interchangeable, and the copyreader's choice is determined by the unit count and by the way the head sounds. "Will" counts one unit more than "To." If "to Speak" and "Will Be Ready" had afforded a better balance of lines, the copyreader would have written the heads that way.

The first three rules for headwriting are accuracy, clarity, and grammatical correctness, and it is sometimes necessary to ignore other principles in order to observe them. Here is a head that is broken into two sentences, instead of flowing as one, but is acceptable because it tells more than a single sentence could:

```
Germ Isolated; Scientists
Link It to Pneumonia
```

Choppiness should be avoided whenever possible, however. This is an unnecessarily bumpy head:

```
Man Wins Suit;
Granted 6 Cents;
Pays $70,000
```

Either of these is better:

```
Man Must Pay
$70,000 for
6-Cent Award
```

```
6-Cent Award
In Lawsuit Costs
Man $70,000
```

Style rules apply to headlines as well as to body copy. Most offices require periods in the abbreviations U.S. and U.S.S.R., and frown on abbreviations that are set adrift, like this one:

```
Homes for Aged
Need Money, Dr.
Tells Committee
```

The prejudice of slotmen affects not only Dr. Tells, but also Rev. Speaks, Gen. Urges, Adm. Orders, Sen. Decries, Sgt. Nabs, and Prof. Snaps.

Style for numbers is sometimes violated in the interest of fitting the head. On most papers, style calls for spelling all numbers under 10, but the headwriter is permitted to use a figure if, for example, 4 or 7 will give him a better fit than "four" or "seven." Because of its scrawny appearance, 1 is usually banned even when other single-digit figures are allowed, and a head that combines styles ("Food Poisons 3 Men, Eight Women") is unacceptable. Some offices also ban heads that start with a one-digit figure, insisting on "Six Colts to Run" instead of "6 Horses Entered."

Punctuation is important to headlines. Since periods are not used, a complete stop is designated by a semicolon. The comma serves its normal purpose and in addition can replace the conjunction "and."

The beginner sometimes assumes that the end of a line replaces punctuation. It doesn't, and these heads wouldn't get by:

```
Masked Man Robs Store        Reds Demand Apology
Flees in Pickup Truck        U.S. Declines Comment
```

The first needs a comma at the end of the line, to replace the missing "and." The second needs a semicolon, to replace the period. Thus they should be:

```
Masked Man Robs Store,       Reds Demand Apology;
Flees in Pickup Truck        U.S. Declines Comment
```

Other headline punctuation follows the usual grammatical rules, except that, as a matter of style, quotation marks are usually single rather than double. Thus it is:

```
Schwartz Attacks Gov. Reagan
As 'Enemy of Public Education'
```

On some papers, the headline comma is not used in figures of less than five digits. Thus the story may report that "3,500" protesting women have demonstrated at the Pentagon, but the headline will say:

```
3500 Women
Protest War
```

Rules on capitalization vary.

A few papers use an all-cap style:

```
FOUR ON SCHOOL BOARD
TO RUN FOR NEW TERMS
```

Some use caps and lower case, capitalizing each word:

```
Four On School Board
To Run For New Terms
```

Some use caps and lower case but do not capitalize prepositions, conjunctions, or auxiliary verbs:

```
Four on School Board
to Run for New Terms
```

Some capitalize prepositions, conjunctions, and auxiliary verbs when they start a line, but not otherwise:

```
Four on School Board
To Run for New Terms
```

And some use a lower case "sentence" style:

```
Four on school board
to run for new terms
```

It's a matter of taste.

The conventions of headwriting—dropping articles, dropping pronouns, using the present tense, etc.—should not be observed slavishly.

The rhythm of the head sometimes requires the article. This is likely to be true if a head is breezily informal, or uses a colloquialism or a common figure of speech. It would be proper for someone to "Steal the Show," rather than "Steal Show," for example, and it would be right for the Mounties to "Get Their Man" rather than "Get Man."

Headlines on features and interpretive stories are often more relaxed and inviting if they use the article. Some examples:

```
McCarthy et al Heat Up a Cauldron

Londoners Wonder
Whatever Became
Of the Summer Sun

A Generation Discovers Jerusalem
```

Features about events of historical significance usually carry heads written in the past tense, and can pick up articles and unessential pronouns as well. Here are a couple of examples, from a Sunday section dealing heavily in interpretive articles about politics and international affairs:

```
The Superintendent Simply Stood Still

Israel Faked Egypt Out of Her Socks
```

The choice of tense is a matter of logic here.

The traditional multideck headline looks like this:

```
Federal Reserve
 Cuts Basic Rate
  On Loans to 5¼%

Reduction of Quarter Point
 in Discount Level Follows
  Interest-Drop Pattern

Board Votes Approval

Move Is Seen As First Step
 in Paring Advances Made
  During Tax-Rise Fight
```

In this design, the first deck, or main head, is known as the "top," and subordinate decks as "drops." They are of different designs. In the example, the top is a stepline head, slanting from left to right. The first drop is an inverted pyramid. It is followed by a crossline and another inverted pyramid.

Other designs are left flush, right flush, centered, and the hanging indentation, which looks like this:

```
New Sources of Revenue Needed
To Meet Higher Budget,
Finance Director Says

New Sources of Revenue Needed
     To Meet Higher Budget,
     Finance Director Says
```

The one-deck headline is predominant in modern headline schedules, however. The most common variation is the readout, a subordinate deck that helps carry the eye from main head to story when the head extends across more columns than the body type. It is used most often with a multicolumn head on the lead story on Page One or the first page of a section. It looks like this:

```
Czechs Defy Kremlin, Vow
To Defend Liberal Policy

             Dubcek Asks
             For Support
             From People
```

Headlines of two decks set to the same measure are also still fairly common. They look like this:

```
  Family Plans
  Camper Trip
  To Far North

Comforts of Home
 Will Go Along
```

Many papers use "kickers." The kicker is a line of smaller type carried above the main headline, usually underlined and usually about half the length of the main head. It looks like this:

```
Formerly in 'Gashouse Gang'

JOE MEDWICK IS ELECTED TO HALL OF FAME
```

The purpose of the subordinate deck and the kicker is to add information. The main head should be written so that it can stand alone, if necessary. The drop or the kicker can either elaborate on what is in the main headline or give new information, but it should not repeat, its content should not be more important than the main headline's, and it should not be used as a crutch to support an incomplete main head.

Many of the rules for the main head also apply to drops and kickers. As illustrated in the examples, the drop is a sentence. The kicker, however, may be a label, lacking even an implied verb, and both the drop and the kicker may depend grammatically on the subject of the main deck, like this:

```
Family Plans
Camper Trip
To Far North

Will Take Comforts
Of Home Along
```

<u>Recalls Days in 'Gashouse Gang'</u>

JOE MEDWICK IS ELECTED TO HALL OF FAME

The most common fault in drops and kickers is the illogical use of an implied subject:

```
Rain Interrupts
Annual Camporee
Of Scout Troops

Orders Boys To Abandon
Tents at Lake Serene
```

<u>Wreck Cars in Sinkholes</u>

STREET CREWS RUSH TO COMPLETE REPAIRS

The copyreader must remember that, while the main head is independent, the drop and the kicker are not. If they don't produce their own subjects, they inherit them from the main headline.

Against this general background, let's take a look at some of the kinds of headline problems, solutions, questions, answers, and errors that can develop in a copyreader's day.

Ambiguity ranks near the top of the list of headwriting hazards. No matter how many rules he learns and observes, any copyreader will write some heads that can be read two ways. He must compress a lot of information into a small space, and he must make identical words and phrases mean different things in different circumstances. He may not "hear" a second meaning that is obvious to someone else.

Prepositional phrases, verbs and nouns with different meanings, and compound modifiers are particularly tricky.

The prepositional phrase:

```
LBJ Defends Policy
On Trips To Bases
```

(Does the phrase "on trips to bases" modify "policy" or "defends"?)

The verb:

```
Reds Warned
Of Air Strike,
Senator Says
```

(Did the Reds warn someone, or did someone warn the Reds?)

The noun of many meanings:

```
Straitsville Now Expected
To Get Water In Spring
```

(The season or the bubbly type?)

The compound modifier:

```
Wild Animal-Hunting Senator
Suffers Scratches on Safari
```

(He should calm down.)

Bad grammar can cause ambiguities like these:

```
Fever of Pope Returns,
Goes Back to Vatican
```

```
Tree Falls
On Man, 29,
Suffocates
```

The lesson is that one word can serve only one master. Neither "Pope" nor "Man" can do a job as the object of a preposition and then moonlight as the subject of a verb.

The telegraphic style of the headline does not give the headwriter license to delete any old word he chooses. Here a strange effect has been created by the arbitrary shortening of a state agency's name:

```
Wildlife to Close
Chillicothe Office
```

And here is a head that fails because a preposition has been deleted:

```
$100,000
Gems Taken
From Home
```

It's supposed to mean that gems with a total value of $100,000 (or $100,000 *in* gems) have been stolen. But it says that gems worth $100,000 *each* are gone.

And in this headline a man named John Corbally was renamed Many Corbally because the copyreader mistakenly thought he could drop "of":

```
Holsinger to Have Many Corbally's Duties
```

The lesson here is that prepositions are not expendable.

Because many words can be either verbs or nouns, the verb head can be strangely ambiguous. Furthermore, if a reader gets accustomed to verb heads he will have a tendency to misread nouns as verbs. Take these three heads, from the same newspaper, as examples:

```
Push Talks
At Chrysler
```

```
Pick Firm
To Survey
City Area
```

```
Report Howl Due in Europe
```

The reader may think that Mr. Push gave a speech, and that the Albert Pick Company is looking for a site for a new hotel. And after learning the truth—that contract talks are being speeded up and that the City Council has selected a planning consultant—he may read the third head to mean that Gen. Howl is about to inspect some troops on foreign soil.

Prohibiting verb heads does not ban heads that begin with a participle or a verb introducing a dependent clause:

```
Lost in Woods,
Campfire Girls
Build Campfire
```

```
Took $40,000
For Vacation,
Teller Says
```

Each of these headlines is clear and has a subject, and therefore is acceptable. Both the participial construction and the dependent clause construction are normally used to save typographical units when the subject-verb-object sequence will not fit. The head at the left, for example, could solve a problem if "Campfire Girls" followed by a comma were a half-unit too long, thus precluding the headline "Campfire Girls,/Lost in

Woods,/Build Campfire." The one at the right solves a problem if the middle line is too long in 'Teller Says/He Took $40,000/For Vacation."

Although a label head can often get along without it, a news head needs a verb. The verb need not always be physically present. Forms of the verb "to be," for example, can be dropped when they are strongly implied. These verbless heads are acceptable:

```
Mayor in Hospital After Heart Attack

Mayor Home from Hospital

Mayor Eager to Return to Work

Mayor Back on Job

Mayor Disappointed by Reports of Aides

Mayor Ready for Retirement
```

The verb should not be dropped if the head is awkward or unclear without it. This verbless head is almost incomprehensible:

```
Step to Avoid
Even Worse
Water Taste
```

The story was about a city council's action to solve a water problem. The head is a label that tries to reflect that. But note that the verblessness is aggravated by the fact that the first word, "Step," while used as a noun, can be read as a verb, and the reader may therefore get the impression that he's being told to leap to the side.

Despite widespread dislike for them, bad splits occur often. They are spawned by miserable head counts, like 9, and then multiply in heads with easy counts.

Here are some bad splits that could have been avoided:

```
Drunk Is Accident-Prone But          conjunction split
Relaxed Condition Is Helpful

Steel Output                         verb split
Continues to
Move Higher

Charged Guy                          modifier split
Wire Kills
Truck Driver
```

Lighting Of Cigarette Causes Crash	preposition split
Man, Two Women Hurt As Cars Collide At Gahanna	conjunction split
Directive Limits Police Questioning of Suspects	modifier split
Symphony Orchestra Will Present Second Concert	verb split
Hoof and Mouth Disease Rampant	modifier split
FBI Nabs 12 In Narcotics Ring	preposition split
Police Arrest Two Men On Theft Charge	modifier split

The copyreader is naturally attracted to abbreviations, but he shouldn't lose his head over them. On well-edited newspapers, only the abbreviations that have been made legitimate by usage are acceptable. Those that are not widely recognized, or are corruptions rather than true abbreviations, are ruled out, no matter how handy. "GOP," for example, is a much used, generally accepted synonym for Republican Party. "GOPs," however, is an illogical abbreviation for "Republicans," and there just isn't any legitimate abbreviation for "Democratic Party" or "Democrats." Newsmen who like the convenience of "Dems" or "Demos" as a headline word would have you believe otherwise, but if they can justify that they can justify Indeps, Socs, Prots, Caths, Ams, Brits, Gers, and any other abbreviation of convenience.

Sometimes they try to do that, and thus speed the acceptance of such corruptions as "prof" and "frat," even though they don't yet endorse "stu" or "sor." Nevertheless, no desk with high standards would pass heads like these:

```
Ohio Wesleyan
Prof To Speak
```

```
Feds End Project
```

```
Official Flays Idea
Of University Rep
```

```
O'seas Servicemen
Receive Aux. Gifts
```

```
Frat Leaders
Plan meeting
```

```
Election Highlights
Press Firm's Convo
```

Some desks accept "Viet" as an adjective or noun applying to all things Vietnamese, north or south, Cong or un-Cong, but those with higher standards resist this sloppy usage lest guerrillas ultimately be said to "viet" a garrison and then vanish "vietly" into the jungle.

Some abbreviations that are banned in copy may be permitted in headlines, if they are generally recognized and often spoken as words. Two examples are "D.A." for "district attorney" and "L.A." for "Los Angeles." States and cities whose names must be used often but are hard to fit into heads are also sometimes abbreviated. "Pennsylvania" and "California" may appear as "Penna." and "Calif.," and "Philadelphia" and "San Francisco" as "Phila." and "S.F." Most editors turn thumbs down on "Philly" and "Frisco," however.

An abbreviation need not be recognized throughout the English-speaking world in order to be legitimate. Local usage makes many short-cuts acceptable. "LVRR" would mean nothing in Fargo, but it would mean Lehigh Valley Railroad to readers of the *Wilkes-Barre Record*. "BN" would mean nothing in Wilkes-Barre, but it would mean Burlington Northern to readers of the *Fargo Forum*.

"Russ" and "rep" and "prof" and "frat" and "convo" and "meet" are corny corruptions that border on headlinese. Allied to them is the corny synonym that would never be seen if there were no headlines. Probably the most common of these is "solon," a word that delights the headwriter because, if he's allowed to use it at all, he can spray it about freely as a synonym for representative, senator, congressman, state senator, state representative, assemblyman, legislator, city councilman, county commissioner, alderman, freeholder, township committeeman, member of parliament, and assorted other public servants. Etymologically, however, "solon" means a *wise* lawmaker.

Because typographical count so severely restricts the headwriter's vocabulary, there is a tendency among copyreaders to take words designed for one purpose and make them serve another. A common device is to use a good verb as a questionable noun:

```
India Favors          Search Widened for Suspect
Disarm Policy         In Kidnap of Former Mayor
```

Most verbs can be either transitive or intransitive, but some are intransitive and that's all. The principle was not understood by the deskman who wrote this:

```
School Bus Bid Meeting Nearly Filibustered
```

And some verbs are just plain transitive, a principle not understood by the deskman who wrote this:

```
Bucks Will Rebound,
Woody Hayes Assures
```

Headwriters sometimes use a word in too broad a context. When Alben Barkley was vice president of the United States, the press referred to him affectionately as "the veep." The word was applied now and then to subsequent vice presidents, but never made much headway as a general term. Copyreaders nevertheless became fond of it as a nice, short synonym for any old vice president:

```
State Board Veep
Raps Dem Policy
```

Here's another example of what can happen when an office permits too much license:

```
Muskie Humphrey's Choice
For Nomination as Veep
```

The headwriter is usually trying to save space when he coins a word, or misuses a word, or uses an archaic or unnatural word. Not always, though. Sometimes he's padding a line, as he was here when he made a stilted substitution for the word "donor":

```
City May Lose
Asian Art Gifts,
Donator Warns
```

And here, where "Foes" was too short and "Enemy Troops" too long:

```
6000 Foemen Slain
In Eight-Day Battle
```

Shades of the World War II copyreader who, remembering President Roosevelt's reference to the "dastardly" attack on Pearl Harbor, habitually referred to Japanese troops as "dastards," as in this classic example of the headline writer's non-art:

```
15,000 Dastards Slain on Bougainville
```

Some copyreaders like to turn nouns, adjectives, and adverbs into verbs, like this:

```
Japanese May Up
Rice Imports from
Red Government
```

It would seem that if they can "up" imports they can also "down" them. The sad thing about this head is that the copyreader didn't have to "up" them to make the words fit. The headline could have said:

```
Japan Considers
Importing More
Rice from China
```

"Local" is a word misused even more in headlines than in body copy. Since it means confined to a limited area, it is incorrectly used in the headline "Local Man Builds Better Wheel Chair." Some newspapers sanction the use of "area" as an adjective to designate a person or thing from the region, as in "Area Soldier Wins Silver Star." But it's best to use the name of the community, or a descriptive term like "county" or "village."

Different offices take different views of the use of slang and colloquialisms in heads. Most, however, would consider this one unconscionable headlinese:

```
Dockers Nix
Grain Appeal
```

And most would reject this, not because the verb is not good colloquial American, suitable in its place, but because its place normally is in the relationship of superior to subordinate, not nation to nation:

```
Rusk Reads Out
Reds For Not
Responding to Aid
```

Possessives sometimes involve subtle problems of usage. Here are two heads written for the same story:

```
Parnell Gets Top Award
At Springfield's Banquet

College President Named
Springfield First Citizen
```

Both err in the treatment of "Springfield." The possessive should not be used in the first, but it is needed in the second. It's basically a question of sound, but a pretty good rule of thumb is to use the possessive when the sense of the phrase is "of," and to drop the possessive when the sense is "in."

"After" is a much abused headline word:

```
Truck Driver, 43, Killed
After Touching Power Line
```

This head implies that the victim touched a power line and then was hit by a car of something. But it means to say that he was electrocuted *when* he touched the power line.

Speaking of accidents, watch out for "mishap." The word connotes a minor incident, a toe-stubber. It's inappropriate here:

```
43 Die, 168 Hurt in Train Mishap
```

Some heads are weak because they are awkward. While grammatically defensible, they just don't sound right. The cause may be that a form of the verb "to be" is missing, either as a main verb or as an auxiliary. It's a hard problem to spot because the verbs of being often are not needed. There is nothing wrong with these heads:

```
Propects Better,
Brokers Report

Three Juniors Elected
To Seats on Council

Leg Broken, Man Crawls
Three Miles to Get Help
```

In the first, the predicate adjective "better" needs no support. In the second, the helping verb "are" is dropped, without damage. In the third, "broken" is a participle, part of an independent phrase, and needs no help from an auxiliary verb.

But now look at three other heads:

```
2000 Evacuated
While Old Bomb
Made Harmless

Giraffes Ride Waves
After Red Tape Snipped

U.S. Pilot Nabbed
After Light Plane
Downed in Cuba
```

All three cry out for a form of "to be": "2000 Evacuated/While Old Bomb/*Is* Made Harmless," "Giraffes Ride Waves/After Red Tape *Is* Snipped," "U.S. Pilot Nabbed/After Light Plane/*Is* Downed in Cuba."

It's one thing to know that the verb improves the sound, and another to understand why. The reason is not implicit in the clauses themselves, because in different circumstances they need no help from the auxiliary. There's nothing wrong here:

```
Old Bomb Made Harmless
After Town Is Cleared

Red Tape Snipped
For Modern Ark

Light Plane Downed in Cuba;
American Pilot Is Arrested
```

If we go back to the first three heads in this section, we see that when the position of clauses and phrases is changed something strange happens to them, too:

```
Brokers Report          Council Posts Are Filled
Prospects Better        As Three Juniors Elected
```

```
Man Crawls For Help
After Leg Broken
```

Now the first headline has become ambiguous; the second and third no longer sound right.

Since the clauses themselves are not at fault, the trouble must stem from the construction of the sentence. And it's not the grammar. "Husband Tight, Woman Holds" and "Woman Holds Husband Tight" are both grammatically correct, as far as headline language is concerned, but they mean rather different things.

If it's not the grammar, it must be the idiom. It would seem that in our idiom a form of "to be" may safely be dropped if it is the main verb or part of the main verb of an independent clause that introduces the headline, but that its omission causes trouble in other circumstances. The headwriter's "idiomatic rule" for this might be: Do not drop a form of "to be" if another verb precedes it in the headline.

Even when he has trouble fitting the words to the typographical count, the experienced copyreader knows what the headline should say. The beginner may not. Troubled by the mechanics of headwriting, he may miss the point of the story, or settle for a head that is incomplete. When Great Britain imposed a livestock quarantine because of an epidemic of hoof-and-mouth disease, one headwriter wrote:

```
Worst Epidemic
In Half Century
Hits British Isles
```

This head missed the point of the story, which was the livestock quarantine and not the epidemic. Worse, the use of "epidemic" without qualification implied a disease in people. The head could have read:

```
Britain Imposes
Rigid Quarantine
On All Livestock
```

When a political candidate whose name had been barred from the ballot objected to being imprisoned in South Vietnam, one headline said:

```
Rejected Aspirant
Protests Jailing
```

This would have meaning only for someone (like the copyreader) who had already read the story. Taken out of context, it is meaningless. Any headline, no matter how difficult the count, must convey some idea of the key elements of the story, even if it cannot tell the story fully. The one above would have had some meaning had it said:

```
Politician Protests
Jailing In Saigon
```

When twenty students were arrested during a civil rights demonstration, a campus newspaper headline read:

```
Arrests Follow Display By U Students
```

But "display" doesn't mean much, and "arrests," without a number, is vague. The head could have said, with greater meaning:

```
20 Arrested During Student Sit-In
```

When a campus critic reviewed the film "Guess Who's Coming to Dinner," the headline said:

```
Reviewer Rates 'Guess Who's Coming to Dinner'
```

But "rates" doesn't tell the reader anything; what else would a reviewer do? The head could have said:

```
Reviewer Pans 'Guess Who's Coming to Dinner'
```

The thoughtless elimination of words can make a head misleading. When the civil rights organization known as ACT announced plans to encourage black businessmen to file petitions in bankruptcy, one newspaper headed the story this way:

```
ACT Planning Campaign
To Encourage Bankruptcy
```

If the headwriter must choose between saying too much and too little, he should say too little. Then he's at least not wrong. For example, suppose the Senate Foreign Relations Committee recommends a $2.5 billion reduction in funds proposed in a foreign aid bill. The copyreader is told to write a two-line, two-column, 48-point Bodoni bold roman head, with a maximum count of 12. Obviously, he can't tell the story completely. So, choosing between too much and too little, he'll do better to lag the ball up to the hole like this:

```
Slash in Aid
Gets Support
```

than to power it too far, like this:

```
Senate Cuts
Foreign Aid
```

Some desks are so careful about overstatement that they will not permit the expression "Miller Guilty" over a story reporting a conviction, insisting instead that the more precise, but longer, "convicted" or "found guilty" be used. Some newsmen argue that a little license should be permitted, that in this case it is understood that "guilty" means the jury's verdict. They have a point, but the verdict cannot change the fact of guilt or innocence. Indeed, many a defendant who has been "guilty" becomes "not guilty" after appeal and retrial. The purists have an edge in this argument.

Accuracy and fairness also require adequate qualification in headlines. Usually, qualification means attribution to a source. It should not be overdone, and it would be ridiculous to write "Storm Rips Valley, *Weatherman Says*," or "Three Hurt in Crash, *Police Say*." But direct or indirect attribution is essential in a headline about an opinion or a disputed issue.

When a National Guard general said he was relieved of command because of his handling of interracial affairs, a headline read:

```
Fired As Guard
CO Because Of
Race Problems
```

Aside from the bad break and lack of a subject, this head is poor because it accepts the general's opinion as fact. It may be, but the writer doesn't know it. The head could have read:

```
Race Problems
Cost Him Job,
General Says
```

This headline has the same flaw:

```
Pacification Program Hurt
But Little by New VC Raids
```

It was written for a story that was based, not on a reporter's first-hand information, but on statements from military sources. It could have read:

```
VC Raids Have Little Effect
On Pacification, U.S. Says
```

A story about an assassination threat carried this headline:

```
6 Youths
May Kill
Wallace
```

The trouble here is the implication that Wallace's life was in imminent danger. The burden of the story, however, was that six young men had threatened to kill him, not that they were likely to carry out the threat.

Too little attribution can also produce "headline editorials." Like these:

```
Democratic Victory
Is Vital to Nation

Johnson Tries to Cover Up Misdeeds
```

These would be all right on the editorial page, but that's not where they came from. They were in the news columns.

The head that editorializes despite attribution is harder to spot as editorializing. Here is one:

```
Education Officer Blames Reagan
For Public Education Regression
```

The head is editorial because it accepts the "regression" of education as a fact, whereas it is only the public education officer's opinion.

Some papers simplify attribution by using the dash and a name, like this:

```
Airport's Future Depends
On Bond Issue — Newell
```

There is nothing reprehensible about the practice, but many offices frown on it because it produces choppy heads and can become monotonous. Once the device is permitted, it is almost certain to be overused.

Some desks also allow attribution in the kicker, like this:

<u>According to Fortune Teller</u>

WORLD TO END TOMORROW

This is poor practice because the main headline, not the kicker, attracts the eye. The kicker is subordinate to and dependent on the main headline, and the main headline should not have to rely on it for meaning.

Overattribution, as in the "weatherman says" and "police say" examples, can be a form of padding. Another form is the use of the time element over a story dealing with the past:

```
Mrs. Harry Carr
Injured Friday
In Auto Mishap
```

```
Southern Dumped
By Central 68-60
Saturday Night
```

The time element is rarely important enough to warrant its inclusion in a present tense headline. Furthermore, when used in conjunction with a present tense active verb, it is always awkward and sometimes anticlimactic:

```
American Scales
Everest Tuesday
```

Names sometimes do nothing but pad a head, and the copyreader who puts a name in a headline should be sure why he's doing it.

Usually, a description like Rockford Dentist, Roswell Woman, or Denver Violinist means more than a name. In deciding whether to use a name or a description, the copyreader is guided by the prominence of the person and by the nature of the newspaper's readership. If the name is generally recognized by readers, it can be used. Otherwise, it should not be. This is often a judgment call. While no headwriter would hesitate to use Kosygin, Humphrey, Mao, or DeGaulle, or the name of the mayor or the school superintendent in his city, or Richard Burton and Elizabeth Taylor, he might be uncertain about using Murphy, Shapiro, Bush, or Evans. When in doubt, he can ask the opinions of colleagues.

Sometimes there is no way to avoid a bumpy, multisentence headline, but before he settles for it the copyreader should take a final look. When a revolutionist spoke bitterly from a jail cell, one headline read:

```
Extremist Jailed;
Assails Captors
```

This can be made into a smooth, single-sentence head with no change in vocabulary:

```
Jailed Extremist
Assails Captors
```

The "So and So Says" headline should be avoided, if possible:

```
Humphrey Says
Campaign Period
Lasts Too Long
```

An easy change:

```
Campaign Period
Lasts Too Long,
Humphrey Says
```

The head that labors the obvious does nothing for anybody:

```
Money Is Essential To Economy
```

Heads, like copy, should avoid the "false passive":

```
Ernest Rattigan
Is Presented With
Tennis Trophy
```

This seems to say that a trophy and Rattigan were handed to someone. Better:

```
Tennis Trophy
Is Presented to
Ernest Rattigan
```

More and more in modern practice, the jump line, or runover head, is not a headline at all but simply a word or two that will guide the reader to the material he wants. Where the story leaves Page One he finds a line like this:

```
See CONGRESS, Page 14, Col. 1.
```

On Page 14, the story is continued under the heading CONGRESS.

Under this system, the copyreader rarely has to worry about the jump head, because the word (CONGRESS, in the example) is usually the story's slug, and it is set in type as a matter of routine, without special instructions from the desk.

Some papers, however, still use the traditional runover head. It is a true headline of one to three lines, complete with verb, and it follows the same rules of language, punctuation, and style as the basic head. On some papers the jump head is a duplicate of the main head. This is nice for the copyreader, but it can cause trouble in makeup because the inside page design does not always lend itself to the kind of makeup that the Page One headline demands. So it is more common to write a separate runover head in a style that meets makeup requirements.

For the sake of the reader, the copyreader should make the jump head resemble the original as closely as possible in content, structure, and vocabulary. If a 60-point, Page One streamer reads

GOVERNOR ASKS $468 MILLION FOR HIGHWAYS

the two-line, 1-column, 18-point runover might read

Governor Asks
Highway Funds

The runover head should never deal with an aspect of the story that is not covered in the main headline. A campus newspaper carried this Page One headline:

Bellow Says DeGaulle Sounded 'Goofy'

The story jumped to an inside page, where the runover head read:

America in Crisis of Confidence, Bellow Says

Small wonder if the reader, turning from Page 1 to Page 6, thought the runover had disappeared.

A Look At the Future

In the 1960s, the newspaper industry finally reacted to the technological explosion. Until then, change had been slow. Wirephoto and Unifax had improved picture coverage of events in distant places, and Teletypesetter had speeded operations (and cut costs) in the composing room. Despite a revolution in other forms of communication, though, the daily newspaper in the United States looked pretty much as it had decades before, and was being produced by techniques essentially the same as those of the late nineteenth century. The American Newspaper Publishers Association had launched a research program, complete with laboratories, but in its early years, just after World War II, even this was aimed primarily at improving the old techniques, rather than (as it would be later) at developing new processes geared to the computer age.

In recent years changes in production systems have been rapid, and while they have not substantially influenced storytelling and copyreading as verbal arts they are affecting the mechanics of reporting and editing in revolutionary ways.

The reporter's traditional disdain for the mechanical aspects of newspapermaking is a luxury the copy editor can't afford, for many of the procedures he is forced to follow, and the problems he faces, result directly from the nature of the newspaper's production operations and the time they demand.

If he is to deal effectively with the inevitable daily surprises, emergencies, and crises, the copyreader must understand the rudiments of the typesetting and printing processes that his paper uses.

While many weeklies and some small dailies are still printed on flat-bed presses, most dailies of any size are produced on high-speed rotary presses by one of two processes: letterpress or offset lithography.

In letterpress printing—still the most common form in newspaper work—paper takes an impression by being pressed directly against a raised surface. The matter to be printed stands in relief on the printing plate and receives ink. The paper touches only this inked surface.

On the rotary press, the curved printing plates are locked onto cylinders. As the cylinders revolve at high speed, paper is fed over them in a "web" from a continuous roll, and is pressed against the plates by adjacent revolving "impression" cylinders. The paper receives impressions on both sides as it moves through these "printing couples" of the cylinders. Finally it is cut, folded, combined with the printed product of other webs, and dispatched from the pressroom by conveyor belt as a finished newspaper.

Offset lithography, sometimes termed photo-offset, involves printing from a flat, rather than a relief, surface. By an adaptation of the principle that oil and water do not mix, ink placed on a photographic plate adheres to the material to be printed and is then transferred to a rubber blanket which in turn transfers or "offsets" the ink impression on paper. Formerly, rotary presses could be used only for letterpress printing, but today they are manufactured for high-speed offset lithography as well.

The typesetting process is of more concern to the copyreader than the printing technique, for the method of composition can determine his deadlines, affect the slugging routine and the procedure for coordinating story and head, and—probably most important—govern the composing room's capacity to handle corrections, adds, inserts, new leads, and late copy on late-breaking stories.

There are basically two typesetting processes: hot and cold. The traditional newspaper system, associated primarily with letterpress printing, uses the hot-type process, in which the material to be printed is cast in relief in lead and then locked into a heavy metal page form. Cold type is set by a photographic process and emerges not as metal standing in relief but as an image on paper. Instead of being placed in a page form, it is pasted onto a sheet the size and shape of a page, then photographed for transformation into a printing plate.

Cold-type composition is used most often in conjunction with offset printing, but not necessarily. Page pasteups can be engraved, just as pictures can, and made into relief plates for letterpress. Similarly, hot type can be used in conjunction with offset printing. After a page is made up, a proof is taken. This is then photographed and made into an offset plate. Or sections of a page can be proofed, and the proofs arranged together, pasted, and photographed.

While letterpress is the traditional newspaper technique, offset printing made tremendous strides during the 1960s, and in the 1970s it may become the dominant process. Early in 1969, the Research Institute of the American Newspaper Publishers Association reported that 405 dailies were printed by offset in the United States, against 1,155 printed by letterpress. But the Institute predicted an almost exact turnover by 1973, forecasting the production of 1,140 dailies by offset and only 420 by letterpress. By 1980, the RI said, offset will be used by 1,376 daily newspapers, letterpress by only 184.

Forecasting developments in newspaper publishing is a risky business. As late as 1966, for example, production experts generally believed that offset printing would not be economical, in the foreseeable future, for newspapers with circulations of more than 70,000, and that the letterpress process would continue to dominate metropolitan publishing for many years. Yet before the decade was over a newspaper with a circulation of half a million—the *San Francisco Chronicle*—was using offset.

Despite the perils of forecasting, it seems safe to predict that advancing technology will change the operations of the newsroom, even if the precise nature of the changes must be left to speculation. The copyreader will find that the revolution in typesetting has more impact on his work than changes in the printing process, for composition is only a step away from him, while printing is further removed. New techniques of data storage and retrieval, made possible by the computer, will also affect the work of the reporter and the copyreader, and will revolutionize the form if not the function of the traditional newspaper library, or morgue.

The accelerating pace of the computer takeover provides a hint, but probably only that, of what may be in store. The computer was first used for hot metal linecasting in 1962, and was adapted to photocomposition in 1964. With the computer came automated hyphenation and justification (spacing out lines so that all are the same length), and the production rate of a hot-type linecasting machine rose spectacularly: from 100–150 lines an hour (or a maximum of about one column in a standard-size newspaper) for manually operated machines, and 200–300 lines an hour for tape-driven equipment, to 500–600 lines an hour. Perhaps as significant is the fact that the computer cut the training time for a machine operator from between two and six years to about two weeks. In cold-type shops, the combination of computer and photocomposition devices has pushed the production rate to thousands of lines per minute.

The computer and linecaster cannot, of course, gather the news, write it, edit it, and compose headlines—although it is certainly conceivable that the computers of the future will be programmed to "write" heads to a variety of counts on the basis of key words fed into them by copy editors, and to do some of the routine chores of editing for punctuation, spelling, and style. (A newspaper that experimented early with computerized editing found that the new technology created a whole new set of problems. Programmed to change "U.S." to "United States" to conform to the style book, the computer instructed the linecasting machine to set an historical reference as "General United States Grant.")

If the problems of finding facts and the words to express them do not change fundamentally as the computer age progresses, the equipment of the reporter and editor certainly will. Reporters on assignment may carry portable teletypewriters that they will be able to link, via telephone lines, directly to a tape-punching device in the newsroom, or to the storage section in a computer. Office typewriters may be set up similarly for tape punching or computer storage.

In that event, the copyreader may either edit the reporter's copy with a pencil and then punch the changes in tape or sit at a console, order the computer to put the story on a tube in front of him, and make his changes on a keyboard or with an electronic light pen. Instead of writing printing instructions—size and measure and type design and so forth—on the copy in longhand, he will probably punch the instructions on a keyboard. By the early 1970s, the wire services and a few newspapers were already making extensive use of the equipment needed for this kind of operation.

Without regard for computer technology, photocomposition alone was bringing about changes in the newsroom by the end of the 1960s. In the cold-type process, for example, proofs cannot be obtained in quantity the way they can in letterpress shops. They must be produced photographically. Some newspapers find that quantity proofing in photocomposition is too costly, and their newsrooms must get along without proofs. This makes it hard to change copy that has been set in type, since the copyreader cannot work at his desk, with a proof, but instead must go to the composing room, find the type or the page pasteup, and make his changes there. For that reason, most stories must be in final form when they leave the copy desk. As a result, photocomposition in its early years has been more popular with low-circulation, single-edition newspapers than with multiple-edition metropolitan dailies, for which the availability of galley proofs and page proofs is essential to the handling of developing stories and the makeover of pages between editions.

Some papers have decided on a gradual transition, switching to photocomposition for some functions while retaining hot-type linecasting for others. Display advertising, for example, adapts itself well to cold-type techniques, and there are shops that use photocomposition for display ads while retaining hot type for news matter and classified advertising.

One of the most promising potential uses for computer technology in the newsroom is in data storage and retrieval. In cooperation with the Massachusetts Institute of Technology, the ANPA Research Institute has experimented extensively with what it calls a "news retrieval system." Under this sytem, articles used in the newspaper are fed into a computer by tape. There they are automatically indexed by using all the words in the lead paragraph, plus all the proper nouns in the story, plus dateline and by-line.

The stories can be "retrieved" at consoles remote from the computer —in the newspaper's library, for example, or in the newsroom, or at a branch office. Instead of going to a clipping file to check background data for a story, the reporter or editor sits at a console and types a "subject phrase." Within seconds, the computer reports back how many articles it has on the subject. The user can then send back additional information—other key words, perhaps, or a dateline—to put limits on the area of his interest, get another report on available material, and sift the stored articles into what he thinks he can use. He can then call for a high-speed printout of the desired stories. When it is perfected, this system will enormously increase the amount of available reference material and will save the reporter and editor much time.

Whatever the coming decade holds in terms of improved technology, it seems doubtful that we are about to reach the point at which the machine will be able to take over the functions of the editor. For while the printed newspaper may be doomed (some predict that the home computer and cathode-ray tube "reader" will replace it), and while it may be possible to "teach" a computer all it needs to know about spelling and style and punctuation and paragraphing and maybe even grammar, the computer may never be able to spot libel, or factual error, or incompleteness, or unfairness, or pomposity, or staleness, or misplaced emphasis, or bad organization, or triteness, or bad taste, or just plain dullness.

The copyreader of the future may be surrounded by gadgetry and never touch a pencil, but he will have a future.

Robert C. McGiffert

Received the A. B. degree in public and international affairs from Princeton and completed master's studies in journalism at Ohio State University. After duty in the Pacific theater during the second world war, he began his news career at the Easton (Pa.) *Daily Express*, which he left after ten years as city editor to join the journalism faculty at Ohio State. He is now Professor of Journalism at the University of Montana, where he teaches news editing, writing, reporting and the law of the press, and he has just completed his second summer as visiting deskman at the *Washington Post.* His wife and two children share his enthusiasm for hiking in the mountains of Glacier National Park, not far from their home.